A Beginner's Guide

to the

Classical Guitar

Jeffrey Goodman

Title   — Shelter of clear light.com
site Sibelus.com   DL "scorch"

Shelter of Clear Light Publishing
Los Angeles

A Beginner's Guide to the Classical Guitar
by Jeffrey Goodman

Front Cover Art: Copyright © 2009 Homa Goodman

The photographs in this book are by Homa Goodman

Shelter of Clear Light Publishing
www.ShelterofClearLight.com

First Edition printed by CreateSpace

ISBN-10   1-4392-6749-9
ISBN-13   978-1-4392-6749-3

Dedication

to our beloved daughter Noosha

Acknowledgments

I wish to extend heartfelt thanks to all of my students,
past, present and future. Without exception, every person
who has ever studied music with me has added vital
substance and life to all that my teaching encompasses.

Also I wish to offer my gratitude to my teachers,
from my long-time mentor Theodore Norman, to my composition teacher
Robert Gross, and to composer and pianist Richard Grayson,
who to this day has generously lent his wisdom, patience,
and his matchless musical sensibility to my musical endeavors.

From my family, particularly my mother and father, I have
never received less than a heartfelt endorsement of my
musical activities, and for that I am grateful beyond words.

From my wife, her patience, passion and unflagging support
have given me the inspiration to persist and continue to
expand my musical horizons.

Table of Contents

PART ONE

Introducing the Guitar

On musicality

The first thing I ask of my new guitar students is to "play something." It is amazing how much guitarists can accomplish and master on their own - even without a teacher, classroom experience, or a general musical background.

How is it possible? Perhaps, I think, it is because even before we start to play an instrument, we *already* intuitively understand music directly and deeply. By the age of two many infants respond to music with astonishing clarity. They easily discriminate between songs they like and dislike. They move and dance in perfect rhythm and happily sing simple melodies.

By adulthood a vast and rich knowledge of music is embedded in our minds: we select styles of music we most enjoy. We have favorite bands, singers, instrumentalists and composers. Among thousands of notes an untrained person can usually, without effort, identify a wrong note or incorrect chord.

Two factors that limit musical growth

Over many years of teaching I have found that people are generally very musical. There are, however, two common limitations that do need to be addressed in order for novices to be successful and fully enjoy their musical endeavors:

1. Lack of solid musical foundation. This means not having encountered and assimilated the basics of music notation, guitar notation and techniques of playing.

2. Lack of a belief in the potential of being *able* to become an accomplished musician or guitarist. Among the thousands of students who have studied guitar with me, it is typical that they underestimate how gifted they are. Perhaps it is because most of us have a rather rooted belief in our limitations, musical and otherwise. A crucial part of teaching music is helping guitarists discover that they can *immediately* do so much more than they ever thought possible.

By providing a solid pathway to the world of classical guitar, this book is offered with the hope that as you embark on your musical journey you will also discover within yourself deeper resources than you may presently imagine to exist. As that process unfolds your initial limitations will be left behind and the true inner gifts of your musicality will come to fruition.

About the book

This musical guidebook is a complete "stand-alone" instruction resource for the first year or two of classical guitar study, and includes basic presentations of fundamentals of music, music notation, guitar notation, right and left hand technique, as well as an extensive repertoire section that contains music organized by both key and level of difficulty.

For centuries all music books were "stand-alone." Since the middle ages a music book on a music stand has been the standard mode of written music transmission. By the 1970s some music books came with cassette tapes, and later on with CDs. Then DVDs.

Today we are at the threshold of a vastly expanding palette of resources that is evolving so fast that even the most cutting-edge musicians and teachers can become breathless just trying to keep up. Classical guitar instruction resources are just now beginning to come to a higher level of fully-integrated multimedia content.

A Beginner's Guide to the Classical Guitar is the central hub that, along with a wide spectrum of multimedia teaching materials, will open many new opportunities for the guitarist to develop.

The multimedia resources include a central information depot at the *Shelter of Clear Light* website, viewable scores with live playback at *SibeliusMusic*, audio recordings of much of the repertoire at *iTunes* and *Amazon*, and video performances and tutorials on *YouTube*.

The multimedia content is scheduled to be released during the course of 2010. Not all, but the vast majority of these offerings, will be free and available to everyone with internet access.

Here is how it works:

1. *ShelterofClearLight.com* - website for all multimedia content

The URL for this site is: *http://www.ShelterofClearLight.com*

After you have the book, you navigate to the *BeginningGuitarGuide* web page of the *ShelterofClearLight* website.

The URL for this page is: *http://www.shelterofclearlight.com/BeginningGuitarGuide.aspx*

There you will be invited to register for automated email notices of content and updates. This is the easiest way to keep up-to-date about everything pertaining to the book and its multimedia resources.

The *BeginningGuitarGuide* web pages will also contain detailed instructions and guidance for all of the multimedia resources. Along with updates and links to multimedia resources, these web pages offer bonus materials that, due to space limitations, couldn't be included in the printed version of the book.

To go directly to the book registration page, navigate on your computer to the URL written below:

http://www.ShelterofClearLight.com/contactus.aspx

2. *SibeliusMusic.com* - website for score viewing and audio playback

Viewable scores with live playback of much of the music and many of the exercises have been and are being uploaded to the music site called *SibeliusMusic.com*.

The URL for this site is: *http://www.SibeliusMusic.com*

Sibelius will invite you to register for their site. Then you will be prompted to download their free viewer called *Scorch*. You are then given full access to view and listen to any of the thousands of scores on their site.

At that point you just navigate to the music you wish to study and begin to listen to the score. (The scores from the book *can* be purchased individually, but since you have the book already you don't need to purchase any of the scores.) You can use the playback controls to play the music, adjust the tempo using a slider, and watch the music as it plays through the sound system of your computer.

This feature of viewable/playable scores addresses one of the tougher parts of learning music. That is: what can a novice guitarist do to figure out *exactly* how the music being studied should sound? Now the solution is easy: go to the musical score on the *SibeliusMusic* site and listen to it while watching the score scroll through the notes. Usually just a few playback sessions will give you the understanding you seek.

(Note that although most of the music will be uploaded to the site, not all of it may find its way there.)

3. *YouTube.com* - website for video tutorials

If you wish to see video tutorials or watch a performance of the piece you are working on, check out the *BeginningGuitarGuide* page of the *ShelterofClearLight.com* website for a list of videos available for free viewing. All of these videos will be uploaded to *YouTube*.

The URL for this site is: *http://www.youtube.com*

Once you have registered to receive our email notifications, you will get an email telling you whenever new videos have been posted.

4. CD recording of repertoire

For an audio recording of the music in the repertoire section of the book, a CD is currently in production. Once the CD has been released, it will be available as a whole, and also as individual tracks, for purchase on iTunes, Amazon, and other internet retailers.

The value of immersion in music

Immersion in music is valuable and easy. For the guitar, go see people play, take some group classes in whatever style appeals to you. For classical guitar, listen to recordings of Segovia, Bream, John Williams, Christopher Parkening and others. Check out the younger generation of players. There are many from around the world who are extraordinary and gifted. Go to *YouTube* and watch videos - amateur, professional, historic. In a few minutes you can find a spellbinding performance of the flamenco master Sabicas, see a young player from across the globe playing Bach in his kitchen, or listen to a group of 50 players who are playing "Flight of the Bumblebee" in a guitar orchestra.

What you need to start

Guitar, preferably nylon string
Music stand
Tuning device
Foot stool
Blank music manuscript paper

It is much more comfortable to learn on a nylon string guitar at first. Steel string guitars tend to be harder on the fingers and the strings are usually more narrowly spaced. If you don't have a guitar yet, see if you can rent one for a few months from a local music shop. That way you can make a more informed choice of a purchase once you have played for a while and better know the direction you wish to take in your music.

Inner inventory

Clear and strong intent
Sense of adventure
Objectivity - different than self-criticism
Patience, persistence
Humility - lack of ego states
Belief in prospects for growth and good results

The inner inventory of what you bring to your music study is much more important than what kind of guitar you are playing. With a clear and strong intent to learn and the resources available for you, a truly great adventure of music discovery awaits all who embark on the journey.

You invest 20% of your effort and your musicality will take care of the rest

The hard won skills of music and playing guitar are neither magical nor inaccessible. There is a natural integration of all musical elements over time. It does take patience and clarity of intent.

Practice creates the impetus to grow and improve. Just by doing and only by doing, do you give your musical ability the chance to put it all together. Your musicality always welcomes your making a connection to it. And it always gives you more than you give it.

Chapter 1

Basic Parts of the Guitar

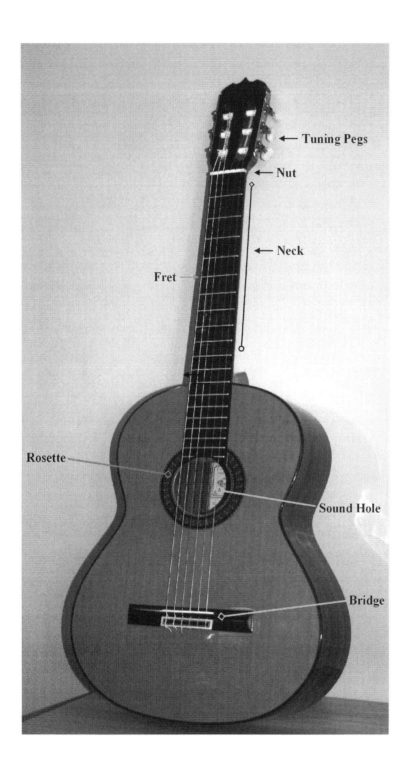

Tuning Pegs

Nut

Neck

Fret

Rosette

Sound Hole

Bridge

In the illustration to the left is a photograph of a classical guitar, with the terms for the main parts of its structure indicated.

In the course of the book these parts are often referred to, so whenever you need to, come back to this page to see what part of the guitar is being discussed.

The guitar pictured was made by José Ramirez in Madrid, Spain in 1984.

Chapter 2
Holding the Guitar

There are many instruction books that give an impression that there is only one "correct" way to sit. That might be true if everyone were the same height, had the same body type, the same hand and finger formation, and the same size guitar, chair and footstool.

What we seek is a natural way of sitting and holding the guitar that allows us to play all the music we wish without being distracted by poor posture or untenable hand positions. Although holding the guitar *looks* simple, even small differences in posture and position effect everything you do on the guitar. The exact way *you* sit will be *unique* to you, yet will draw upon some of the principles outlined below.

Before Sitting

Before sitting, stand up straight with your hands at your sides and breathe in and out a few times. Loosen up your arms and shoulders. Gently rotate left and right just a bit to fully relax the body. This way, when you sit you will have already created a grounded sense of relaxation.

Sitting

1. Sit on a comfortable straight-backed chair, towards the front edge. Lean slightly forward. Center your upper body weight over the hip bones. (Do not lounge back in the chair.) Then place a foot stool so you can elevate the left leg about 4-10 inches. You may adjust the foot stool for comfort at any time.

2. Balance the guitar over your left thigh and lean the guitar slightly towards you. This helps create a line of sight so you can see the strings and frets of your guitar.

3. The neck of the guitar should be elevated above the horizontal. If the neck is parallel to the floor it is much harder for the left hand to play.

4. Keep your lower back straight. If you hunch down your breathing will be constricted.

5. Place your right foot a little back and under the seat of the chair.

6. If you can stand up easily you are in a dynamic sitting position. If you have to adjust your body before you can stand up, you will need to experiment with how you are sitting a bit more.

Take time to explore your sitting position. Everything that happens at your fingertips is subtly influenced by how you are sitting. Expect to have a some back and shoulder discomfort initially as you learn to play. Make adjustments and over time these beginner's aches will disappear.

Your body is as important a teacher as any you will ever encounter. It always supplies you with signals for both when you need to revise an action and when what you are doing is on the right track.

Playing well always feels better than playing poorly. An amazingly rich spectrum of physical sensations are an intrinsic part of being a guitarist.

Right Arm and Hand

1. While supporting your guitar with your left hand, and with the guitar resting on your left thigh, completely relax your right arm, letting it drop to your side. Then lift your forearm by flexing from your elbow, with your wrist fully relaxed, and then rest the forearm lightly on the upper side of the guitar.

2. Rotate your wrist slightly so that your fingertips point towards the strings. Depending on your height and the length of your arm, your fingers will be within a few inches of the sound hole. Taller people will have their fingers naturally pointing to the strings more toward the fretboard, and shorter people will have their fingers pointing over the sound hole or a little ways towards the bridge.

3. Now adjust where your forearm is resting on the top of the guitar so that your fingers are just "behind" the sound hole, with the thumb extended past the rosette and into the space above the sound hole. (See the lower illustration on this page.)

4. The wrist is slightly bent. This helps to prevent undue tension within the fingers and promotes good contact points of the nails and strings.

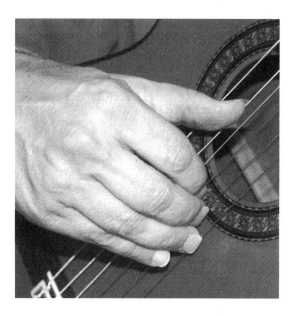

5. The knuckles are kept roughly parallel to the strings. This orientation will *change* depending on the musical texture. For tremolo and scale playing the parallel line of the knuckles to the strings is helpful. For chords and arpeggios the knuckles adjust to a slight angle to the strings. (Don't try to over-control this aspect of technique. Your body will naturally make any necessary adjustments for you. This works very well for everyone, unless the player keeps his fingers in a tense posture. In that case the body cannot make subtle and fluid adjustments.)

6. The fingers are curved just enough to contact the strings.

7. The thumb is extended away from the action of i, m and a. Otherwise the thumb will tend to bump into the other fingers. When that happens, just re-position the thumb by extending it again towards the middle of the sound hole. The tip of the thumb contacts the string at roughly a 45 degree angle. If the thumb is positioned parallel to the string it will tend to produce a fuzzy and unfocused tone. The angled approach makes a better tone and also makes it easier to pluck all the bass strings.

Left Arm and Hand

1. While supporting your guitar with your right arm, completely relax your left arm, letting it drop to your side. Then lift your left arm away from your body and slide your hand along the neck of the guitar, with the thumb behind the neck and your other fingers moving along in front of the strings.

2. When you have positioned your hand at the area of where the frets begin, place the thumb in the middle of the back of the guitar neck. (Use the lower illustration on this page as a visual reference.)

3. The wrist is bent just enough to allow the fingertips contact with the strings.

4. In general, the fingers are kept curved rather than straight.

5. When you press down any string to make a note, without any forcing, try to guide the fingertip to an angle *towards* a perpendicular to the fretboard. When the fingertip is pressing from that angle it requires much less pressure to hold the string down. The human hand is a miracle of engineering, so *let it guide you* to effective finger placement. Never attempt to force your fingers or hand to an artificial concept of "correct" posture. That will only hold you back in your progress, and there is no virtue accumulated by imposing an artificial ideal that does not enhance your potentials as a guitarist.

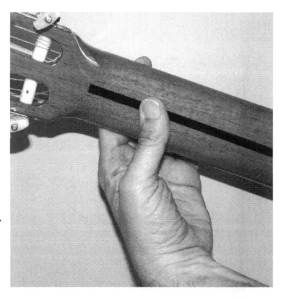

6. If the fingertips are not relatively perpendicualr to the fretboard, it requires more pressure to hold down the note. Even so, when your fingers play the bass string notes, they *must* straighten somewhat in order to reach them. In that case a *slight* bend at the first joint is all that is needed to make a good contact and musical tone.

7. Whenever possible, each finger will cover the territory of one fret. The first finger plays notes in the first fret, the second finger plays notes in the second fret, and so forth.

This chapter on holding the guitar, right and left arm and hand positioning, is developed and expanded as the book unfolds. All guitarists study these subjects throughout their musical lives.

Chapter 3
Basics of Music Notation

A Glimpse of History

Early in the 11th century a Benedictine monk named Guido of Arezzo wished to assist his church choir in their singing of Gregorian chants. This led to his invention of a method of writing music that is the basis of the notation system that we use today.

Developed by musicians over almost one thousand years, staff notation is the universal mode for representing music.

The two most important elements of music notation are pitch and duration. First we will discuss pitch notation: that is - names of notes, their symbols and how they are represented:

Notes

Notes are named after the first seven letters of the alphabet:

A B C D E F G

Notes are placed on a *staff* (the higher the pitch, the higher it is placed on the staff) using a symbol called the *notehead*.

The notehead can be either:

  1. a hollow oval: 𝅝
  2. or a filled-in oval: ●

The Staff

The staff is a five-line graphic matrix that notes are placed in:

Treble Clef →

The guitar uses the treble clef to notate music for the guitar. The treble clef is placed at the beginning of each line of music and fixes the note "G" on the second line of the staff:

Treble Clef →

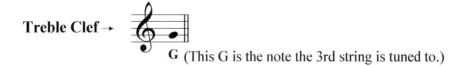

G (This G is the note the 3rd string is tuned to.)

Notes on the Staff

The notes are placed on the lines or in the spaces of the musical staff:

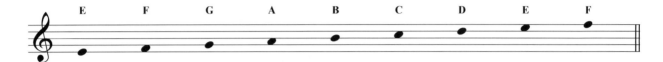

Many find it helpful to divide the notes within the staff to notes on lines and notes in spaces.

notes on lines:

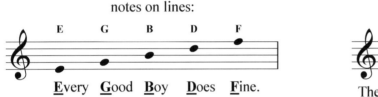

Every Good Boy Does Fine.

The notes on lines can be memorized using
the mnemonic above.

notes in spaces:

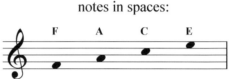

The notes in spaces spell the word *FACE*.

Ledger Lines

Notes that are higher or lower than the staff are notated with small lines, called *ledger* lines, that
in effect *extend* the staff just for that note:

Musical Intervals

In music the term *interval* means the musical distance between two notes.

The Half-Step

The smallest interval is called the 1/2 step. On the guitar a half-step is formed between any two notes
on adjacent frets of a string. Also, a 1/2 step is formed between any open string and the first fret of
that string.

Accidentals

The signs which raise, lower, or alter the pitch of a note are called accidentals. Accidentals modify the pitch of the note they come before by 1/2 step:

♭ ← This is a flat: It *lowers* the note by 1/2 step or 1 fret.

♯ ← This is a sharp: It *raises* the note by 1/2 step or 1 fret.

♮ ← This is a natural: It *removes* the sharp or flat of the note.

Key Signatures

Sharps and flats at the beginning of a piece are used throughout the piece. This is called the key signature. The key signature can indicate *either* a major or a minor key.

Further study of music theory will help you determine which key, major or minor, is associated with a given key signature. Below are examples of common key signatures that the guitar plays in:

G major	D major	A major	E major	F major
the note F is sharped	the notes F & C are sharped	the notes F, C & G are sharped	the notes F, C, G & D are sharped	the note B is flatted

The Octave

The *octave* is the interval spanned by two notes, where the higher note is twice the frequency of the lower note. The sound of both notes is so close to being identical that they are given the same letter name. This is why the seven letter names of the notes (A → G) are *repeated* as they cycle throughout the staff.

Staff notation has a unique position for each note we play. Study the example below and observe each pair of notes. The boxed pairs show octaves created with the notes named E. Visually the octave always is written with one note in a space, and its octave pair on a line, with 2 and 1/2 spaces between them.

Octave pairs on the guitar:

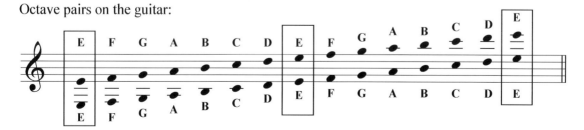

Time Value of Notes

The mapping of durations, or the time value of notes, is another crucial aspect of music notation.

A Common Misconception

Many novice musicians feel that they lack "rhythm ability" because of the time required to master rhythm notation. Yet almost everyone has an innate sense of rhythm. Musical rhythms are reflections of how humans breathe, move, laugh, speak, and sing.

What does take effort and plenty of patience is learning to interpret the notation for rhythm. When we contemplate the miraculous precision of rhythm notation, and its capacity to map rhythm structures for every style and combination of instruments, it should be no surprise that fluency in reading rhythms is a precious journey shared with all other trained musicians. It does not happen in a blink of an eye.

Even if the top innovators of Google or Microsoft decided to produce the ultimate instruction book on musical rhythm, every person would still have to learn by doing. If you remember learning to ride a bicycle, your success was not based on what someone told you, or reading a book. You kept trying until you got the hang of it. Then it was easy. Rhythm notation is just like that.

How Rhythm is Notated

Rhythm is notated using symbols that are attached to or next to the symbols for pitch. The chart below names the basic symbols, shows what they look like, and gives the number of counts that each symbol gets.

Kind of Note	What It Looks Like	Number of Counts
Whole Note -----------------------------	o	**4** quarter note counts
Half Note -----------------------------	♩	**2** quarter note counts
Quarter Note ----------------------------	♩	**1** count per quarter note
Eighth Note ---------------------------	♪	**2** counts to a quarter note
Sixteenth Note ------------------------	♬	**4** counts to a quarter note
Thirty-second Note ----------------	♬	**8** counts to a quarter note

The example below illustrates notes with different rhythmic values placed on the staff:

Measures and Bar Lines

Music is divided by vertical lines called bar lines into portions called *bars* or *measures*. Both words mean the same thing.

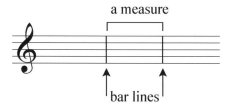

Time Signatures

A time signature consists of two numbers shown at the beginning of the music.   The upper number tells how many beats are in each measure. The lower number indicates the kind of note that gets one beat.

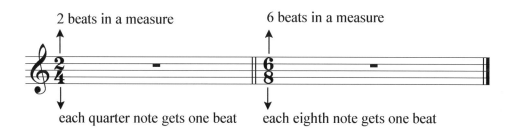

Beams and Flags

Notes with flags may be joined together with beams. The flag and corresponding beam have the same rhythmic value:

Rests

Each note has a corresponding rest which is counted in the same way as the note.

The Tie

A curved line connecting two notes of the same pitch is called a tie. Only the first note of a tie is played, the value of the second note is added to it. The arrows below point to the ties that lengthen the initial notes:

Dotted Notes

A dot placed after a note adds to the time value of the note by half its value:

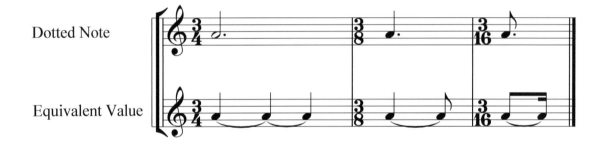

Triplets

Three notes of equal length in one beat is called a triplet. A triplet can be applied to any note value. Here below are a few of the most common triplets:

The triplet is shown with the number "3" centered above or below the three note group. The triplet can be notated with or without accompanying brackets.

Mastering Rhythmic Structures

All elements of rhythmic notation are mastered through practice. When you are ready, begin to study Chapter 13, called Basic Rhythm Exercises. It will guide you to a deeper understanding of all the elements of rhythm notation introduced here.

Additional Elements of Music Notation

On this page you will find a few more commonly encountered elements of music notation.

Double Bar

A double bar signifies the end of the composition or a portion of it:

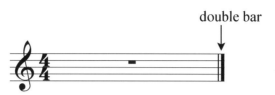

Repeat Signs

A repeated section of music is indicated by a double bar with added dots.
(If there is no "start repeat" sign it means to repeat to the very beginning of the music.)

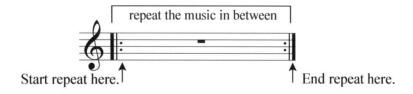

First and Second Endings

Sometimes a repeated passage has a different closing when played for the second time.
The 1st ending is played only the first time. When playing the repeat do not play the
1st ending, rather skip directly to the bracketed music that shows the 2nd ending.

A Hint about Working with Music Notation

This chapter illustrates the most essential elements of music notation. Use this section as a reference
when you wish to identify a symbol or element of music notation you are working on.

What you study in this chapter is applicable to music for *any* instrument or voice. Used in conjunction
with Chapter 4 on Guitar Notation, over time it will become second nature for you to pick up any guitar
piece and just begin to play.

Chapter 4

Guitar Notation

Music notation maps the pitch and duration of all the notes of a piece of music. Music notation, by itself, is universal: everyone who reads music can understand the notes in the example below. Most instruments have special additional notations which give information needed to play that instrument. Guitar notation has many elements. The most important are outlined below.

 ← Look at this example of pure music notation. Until guitar notation is added, there is no way to know which strings or fingering to use.

Guitar notation, added to music notation, shows what strings and fingers to use to play the notes. Guitar notation consists of symbols for left and right hand fingers, the guitar strings, and the *position* to play in.

Left Hand Notation

Fingerings for the left hand are indicated with numbers:

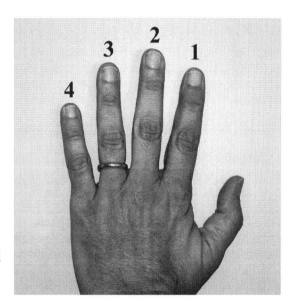

1 = **index finger**
2 = **middle finger**
3 = **ring finger**
4 = **small finger**
0 = **open string** *

* Open String

An *open string* is when the note to be played is plucked by the right hand *without* using the left hand. The sound made, of course, is the pitch that the string is tuned to. The notation for an open string is the symbol "0" → **0**

Right Hand Notation

Fingerings for the right hand are indicated with letters. They are derived from the Spanish words for the fingers, although we use the letter "*s*" for the small finger.

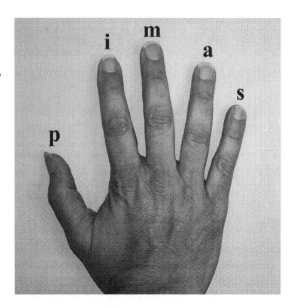

p = **thumb**
i = **index finger**
m = **middle finger**
a = **ring finger**
s = **small finger**

The small finger of the right hand is only used in flamenco music. Chapter 28, on <u>Flamenco,</u> illustrates the *rasgueado* strum that uses the small finger.

String Notation

Each string is named by the *note* to which it is tuned and is numbered as follows: the high E string is called the 1st string, the B string is called the 2nd string, etc. When you see a circle with a number in it, that tells which string the note is to be played on. For example: the symbol: ③ means to play the note on the 3rd string. Study the fretboard diagram below to see how this notation works:

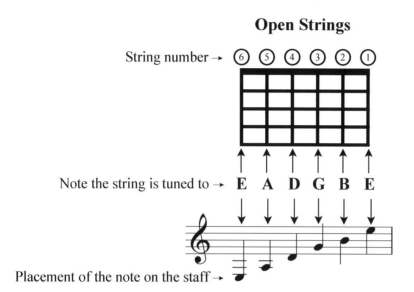

Open Strings

String number → ⑥ ⑤ ④ ③ ② ①

Note the string is tuned to → **E   A   D   G   B   E**

Placement of the note on the staff →

Notation of *Position* for the Left Hand

The term *position* refers to *where* on the fretboard your left hand is stationed. It is defined by which fret the left hand index finger is oriented to. When the index finger is playing the *first* fret of any of the six strings the hand is said to be in the *first* position. In the first position the left hand spreads each of its fingers, one for each fret, from the 1st to the 4th fret. As long as the 1st finger is oriented to the first fret of any string, that is the first position.

Roman numerals are used to indicate position. That is: **I = 1st position**
                                                        II = 2nd position, etc.

The "hollow" circles with numbers in the fretboard example below show where the fingers *can* be placed within the 1st position. The *region* of the 1st position notes is diagrammed below:

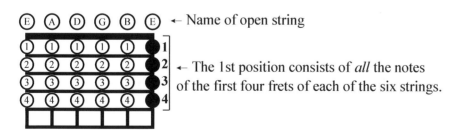

← Name of open string

← The 1st position consists of *all* the notes of the first four frets of each of the six strings.

I ←The roman numeral indicates which position the notes are to be played in.

←The notes F → G# are 1st position notes of the 1st string. They are notated in the diagram above by the black dots, with the fingers offset to the right.

13

To further illustrate the concept of position, look at this diagram below of notes in the 5th position:

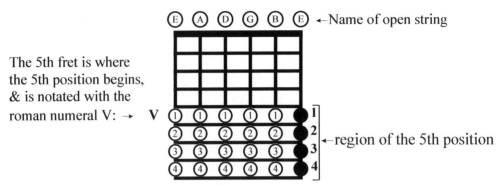

The 5th fret is where the 5th position begins, & is notated with the roman numeral V: →

←Name of open string

←region of the 5th position

The notes A → C are played on the 1st string, starting in the 5th position: →

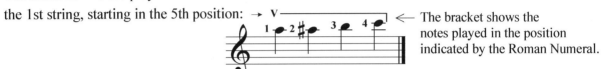

← The bracket shows the notes played in the position indicated by the Roman Numeral.

At first you will be learning music almost entirely in the 1st and 2nd positions. Many novices assume that the higher positions are more difficult to play in. Actually, if anything, they are easier to play *once* you know the note locations. Higher positions are easier because the higher frets are closer together and the fingers do not have to stretch nearly as much along the horizontal axis of the strings.

For now, begin to work with the concept of position playing without trying to fill in every detail. Below are the first three measures of the melody of J. S. Bach's *Jesu Joy of Man's Desiring*. Example one contains complete fingering notation for the 1st position. The 2nd example is notated for playing in the 2nd position.

Example 1: in the 1st position:

Example 2: in the 2nd position:

The 2nd fret is where the 2nd position begins, & is notated with the roman numeral II: → **II**

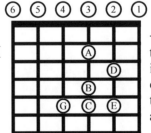

←This diagram shows where the melody notes are played in the 2nd position. Of course, this melody is easier to play in the 1st position as shown above.

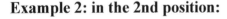
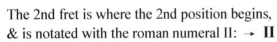

14

Chapter 5

Map of Notes on the Guitar

About the Map

Within just a few minutes a beginning piano student can learn to find any note by name on the piano. For the guitarist that same skill can take many years to learn.

The guitar has a more elusive design, but that should not obstruct the useful knowledge of where notes are on the fretboard.

After centuries of evolution, the guitar we use today has six strings, with four of the adjacent string pairs tuned four notes apart, and one string pair tuned three notes apart. Each string is divided by frets, so that one string can play nineteen (or more) different notes. This design makes finding notes on the guitar somewhat complicated, and can be an obstacle to novice guitarists.

It is no wonder that guitarists tend to shy away from music notation. Even so, the benefits of learning to read music on the guitar are so great that the effort is one of the best investments of time any guitarist can make.

The *Map of Notes on the Guitar* graphically shows everything a guitarist needs in order to connect music notation to where the notes are to be played on the guitar.

It graphically associates and translates music and fretboard notations so that any natural note within the first twelve frets may be easily found.

Once the underlying concept of how the guitar is organized to play notes is mastered, it is a small and easy step to extend fretboard knowledge to include all notes on all frets, including chromatic notes and the highest regions of the fretboard.

It will save a lot of time if you make a photocopy of the main map page and place it nearby the music you are working on. The map can be used with any music.

Map of Notes on the First 12 Frets of the Guitar

How to use the Map of Guitar Notes

How the Map Works

1. The Map is divided into six sections, one for each string on the guitar. Each section has an upper and lower part.

2. The upper part of each section has standard music notation for all the natural notes on the string up until the 12th fret.

    a. Above each note is the letter name of the note.

    b. Next to each note is a number, from 0 to 12, which tells which fret the note is played in. (The "O" means play the open string to sound that note.)

3. Beneath the staff notation is a fretboard diagram which is lined up beneath the notes shown on the staff. There is a black dot with a letter name of the note that is played in that fret location. It is always the same as the note shown in the staff above.

A Few Exercises Using the Map to Find Notes

1. Play a natural scale ascending and descending on each open string, using the map on page 16 as a guide. Visualize and name the note as you play, observing the fret location of each note.

2. Study the examples below of the note F, and the note D, and use the map to find and verify the primary and secondary locations of these notes. Afterwords, choose various notes and repeat the process until you can readily navigate the map to find any note you wish.

This note F can be found on several strings:

Use the map to find the note D on the 2nd, 3rd and 4th strings:

Best Use of the Map of Guitar Notes

Keep in mind that once you have focused your *intention* to learn the notes on the guitar you will have created a potent force for success. Although the learning does not come with the speed of a fast food item through a take-out window, the knowledge and mastery of music notation acts to enhance every aspect of your music making on the guitar.

Chapter 6
Tuning the Guitar

Introduction to Tuning the Guitar

Tuning a string to its correct pitch involves both an internal and an external process. The first and most essential part of tuning takes place when the guitarist *listens* to a standard pitch source. It can be a tuning fork, a pitch pipe, a piano, another guitar, or any sound source that has a correct pitch. The human sense of hearing is so precise that our ears can instantly detect even a small fractional difference between two pitches. Pitch sensitivity is a foundation for all of music. Novice guitarists can begin a lifelong internal process of deep listening: inner listening forges a link between you and the guitar you play.

Electronic Tuners

Today's technology has produced electronic tuners that effectively bypass the musician's act of listening. Using lighted reference guides, meters or arrows, these tuners, in effect, *listen* for you. When an open string is played, the tuner analyzes that pitch and signals whether the string is:

1. in tune
2. flat (too low in pitch)
3. sharp (too high in pitch)

If the note is shown to be sharp or flat, the guitarist adjusts the pitch until the tuner detects a match of frequencies. It then shows something like a green light, or the meter's indicator wand centers on the "in tune" line of the display.

Relative Tuning

Relative tuning means tuning the guitar to itself, so that all the strings are the correct distance in pitch from one another. This is how people tuned centuries ago. In fact, each town or city during the time of J. S. Bach is known to have had different calibration frequencies for their music. Everyone in the town orchestra would tune according to the pitch of the local church organ.

There may be times today when your tuner isn't around, there is no piano handy, and yet you still wish to play. Relative tuning always works and is not difficult to master.

Adjacent strings are all tuned 4 tones apart, except that the G string is 3 tones apart from the B string:

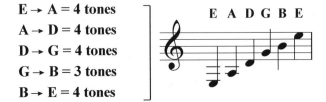

E → A = 4 tones
A → D = 4 tones
D → G = 4 tones
G → B = 3 tones
B → E = 4 tones

E A D G B E

Using the diagram and the step-by-step instructions below, try using relative tuning to tune your guitar. Begin with the low E string, then proceed until you have tuned the high E. After tuning, take out your electronic tuner and check your tuning string by string. Then, if necessary, make small adjustments until *both your ear and the tuner* are in agreement.

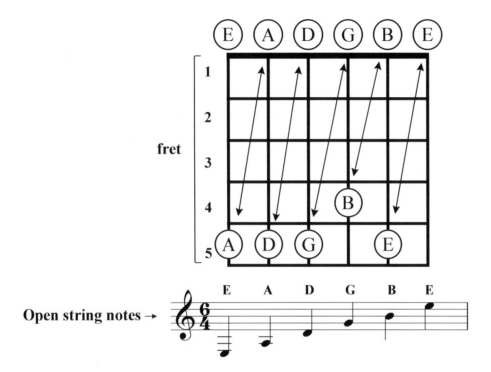

Open string notes →

Step-by Step Instructions for Relative Tuning

1. If possible, check out the low E (it is ok to use the tuner or tuning fork) to see if the pitch is correct.

2. Press the 5th fret of the 6th string to produce the note A.
   Tune the 5th string to a *unison*. (Unison means exactly the same pitch.)

3. Press the 5th fret of the 5th string to produce the note D.
   Tune the 4th string to a *unison*.

4. Press the 5th fret of the 4th string to produce the note G.
   Tune the 3rd string to a *unison*.

5. Press the 4th fret of the 3rd string to produce the note B.
   Tune the 2nd string to a *unison*.

6. Press the 5th fret of the 2nd string to produce the note E.
   Tune the 1st string to a *unison*.

More on the Art of Tuning

Learning to tune will deepen the pleasure of playing and listening to music. It also improves the accuracy of your hearing. But it does take time and experimentation to become good at it.

The following techniques facilitate rapid improvement and mastery of tuning:

1. After playing the correct pitch from a sound source (piano, another guitar, tuning fork, etc.) *sing* this pitch aloud. If the pitch is an E, sing the pitch using its name: that is sing "*Eeee*". This focuses your awareness on the pitch and actually fosters a kind of inner bodily tuning to the pitch.

2. After playing the string to be tuned, ask yourself whether the string is:

   a. higher than
   b. lower than
   c. the same as the standard pitch.

3. If you are not sure what the relationship is between the two pitches, try loosening (hence lowering) the string you are tuning until you are sure that it is *lower* than the standard pitch.

4. Now adjust the string by tightening it (making is sharper) until it produces a clear unison with the standard pitch.

5. Once you have done the above on each of the strings, try strumming an E major chord. (See Chapter 11 on Guitar Chords for how to play the E major chord.) If everything sounds good to your ear, go ahead and play. If the chord sounds a little off, find the string or strings which seem not to "fit" and retune those strings until the chord sounds harmonious.

6. One of the best approaches to tuning is to first tune the low E string with an electronic tuner. Then, using relative tuning, tune the rest of the strings. Finally, with the electronic tuner check your tuning again, of *all* the strings. This gives you instantly precise feedback and corrections. Your musical intuition will absorb the whole process and over time the accuracy of your tuning will equal or even surpass the tuner itself.

If may seem paradoxical, but the players who are most frustrated with the tuning of their guitar usually have extremely precise pitch awareness. That is why even small inaccuracies are so irritating. (As a child Mozart was said to occasionally faint if he heard a loud sound that was out of tune.)

Also keep in mind that tuning is a *continuous* process during guitar playing. Even when you start off with a good tuning, as the guitar is played, the strings dynamically change their pitch and need small adjustments.

As with many aspects of learning guitar, a relaxed patient awareness and clear attention to each issue eventually prevails. *Water, as it passes over rough stones in a stream, does not get frustrated at the lack of smoothness of the stones beneath.* With time your musical intuition integrates all the elements you need to advance your playing.

Chapter 7
The Art of Practicing

The quality of your practice, and the amount of time you invest, combine together to help you grow into the kind of musician and guitarist you wish to become.

Fine musicians - just like top athletes - develop and maintain their skills in a comprehensive and systematic way.

As you begin to develop your guitar technique the task of just getting your body to physically carry out basic guitar skills is daunting enough. Nevertheless, it is rare that guitarists are defeated by their physical limitations. Much more common is that guitarists do not nurture themselves with the gift of becoming good musicians. Guitarists who have not developed their musicianship can only sporatically transcend the mere physical transmission of sounds and really appeal to the hearts and spirits of the people they play for.

The great English guitar virtuoso Julian Bream, in introducing his master class in San Francisco in the early 1980s, said "I am *not* a guitarist. Rather, I am a musician who plays the guitar."

There are many who play the guitar with excellent skill, but far fewer who, when they play, transmit and share a charismatic vision of the music they are performing.

As you begin the journey of learning to play guitar, it is deeply influenced by your intention to delve into the all aspects of music and instrumental technique. With this in mind, consider the following guidance and problem-solving tips for your practice. Many of the questions that will arise as you are learning to play can be addressed by applying what is offered here.

1. Play your guitar every day. Even if only for a few minutes. Your musicality is activated *every* time you play. Just getting your guitar out and playing a simple piece or a scale stimulates your musical subconscious to work for you, and your musical mind will continue its processing later on, even when your thoughts and activites are on other matters. Think of your musical subconscious as an ally that can be easily turned on, like a light switch. Just taking your guitar out of its case essentially flips the switch on. Please don't forget to do it!

2. Work in short time periods, rather than marathon sessions. For each fifteen minutes of playing, take a short rest. This clears your mind and lets your muscles relax after being worked.

3. Take small and easy steps. For example, it is better to work for a time on a few of the chords in the key of C major, rather than on the whole set of chords presented in the chapter on basic chords. If you get tense or frustrated during practice, maybe you are trying to do too much too soon. When that happens, consider how to reduce your point of focus. You will be able to sense when the scope of your work is about right.

4. Establish a specific goal or focus for each day's work. For example: "On Monday I will work on memorizing the D minor scale. On Tuesday I will then sight read in the key of D minor, using the scale memorized on the previous day."

5. <u>Design and follow a practice plan</u>. There are many approaches to the design and content of daily practice. Here is a sample one-hour session:

    a. **Warm-up**   (10-15 minutes)
       Scales
       Right hand exercises
       Left hand hammer-on and pull-off exercises

    b. **Sight Reading**   (10-15 minutes)
       Single-note melodies
       Chord progressions in a given key
       Arpeggio studies

    c. **Repertoire**   (20-25 minutes)
       One new piece
       One older piece, with a focus on memorization

    d. **Review**   (10-15 minutes)
       Technical materials such as scales of thirds, natural harmonics, etc.
       Previous repertoire

6. <u>Vary your routine occasionally</u>, yet keep a balance in terms of what you cover. It is neither possible nor desirable to cover every exercise and piece during each session. If you find that your mind wanders when you approach a particular subject matter, perhaps let it go for a while. Substitute another element you wish to explore, and then after a time return to what you have set aside. Usually the mind, after a break, is more than willing to get back to work and the old resistance will have disappeared.

7. <u>Learn to evaluate your own practice</u>. If something you are doing is yielding good results, expand that activity. If something you are doing seems to be leading nowhere, set it aside with the intention of returning at a later time when you may be more ready for that subject.

Common Problems: Their Causes and Cures

Incorrect and faulty finger placement is a shared issue for everyone who learns to play guitar. Some of the most fundamental causes and corrections are outlined below:

Buzzes

When the note you play makes a buzzing kind of sound, there are only a few causes. The cure is usually simple.

Cause #1: Left hand finger placement is too far behind the fret.

Cure: Place the finger just behind the fret whenever possible.

Cause #2: The right hand plucks the string before the left hand is set.

Cure: Wait until the left hand finger has the string firmly down, then let the right hand pluck the string.

Muted Sounds

Muted sounds are very common for the beginning player. Here are the main causes and cures:

Cause #1: The left hand finger is placed directly on top of the fret.

Cure: Move the finger back until it is just behind the fret.

Cause #2: A left hand finger is leaning against the string to be sounded. This often happens with chords.

Cure: Increase the curvature of your finger until it clears the muted string.

Choppy Sound

To transform choppy, disconnected sounds into smoother, more evenly-flowing sounds:

1. Be sure to <u>leave the left hand fingers down</u> for the full duration of the note. This applies especially to bass notes.

2. <u>Alternate right hand fingers</u> on the melody notes. Using the same finger for several notes in a row is to be avoided whenever possible.

3. <u>Learn to anticipate</u> the next action within the chain of successive actions. This helps eliminate sudden, uncontrolled gestures. Smooth sound can only be created by smooth physical actions.

4. <u>Memorize the passage that is choppy</u>. Memorization helps you organize the physical and musical aspects of playing so that the music flows in the best possible way.

How to Work on Trouble Spots

Everyone who learns to play an instrument has the experience of working on a passage which just will not come together. Before giving it up entirely, or merely repeating it with flaws and mistakes, try the following practice tools:

1. Identify the issue

The precise diagnosis of the *exact* point of difficulty is the first step towards a solution. Use a pencil to mark each spot of the music that you have difficulty with. The more clarity you bring to identifying the nature of the hard spot, the more likely a solution will be forthcoming. Here are a few of the most common recurring types of trouble spots.

    a. Not knowing the notes.
    b. Not keeping to the rhythmic design.
    c. Left or right hand fingerings either awkward or undefined.
    d. Chord with unfamiliar or difficult fingering.
    e. Difficult shift required of the left hand from one position to another.

Each difficulty is an opportunity for you to expand your musical mastery. Your musical intuition will actually identify and correct many trouble spots for you without much conscious probing on your part. However, if a spot remains difficult after you have practiced a passage for a reasonable amount of time, learn to analyze the fine details of the passage as deeply as you can. Everything you discover is added to your repertoire of problem-solving tools. And when you solve a tough problem it naturally increases your confidence that you can indeed master guitar technique.

2. Divide into small segments.

Divide the section into small units, even if they are each just two or three notes or chords. This helps you to specify the exact nature of the technical issue.

3. Slow tempos

Play more slowly than you think you need to. Often we try to play too fast too soon. When the passage is firmly established at the slower tempo, gradually increase the tempo.

4. Memorization

Memorize the passage you are studying. This will allow you to devote your full attention to the instrumental technique you are trying to solidity. When you are reading the music note by note you will not be able to concentrate fully on the physical aspects of playing.

Applying the above practicing techniques will lead to resolution of many difficult passages. If you still find the passage too difficult, it may at the moment just be too hard for you. Set it down, return to it later - after a time you will be able to solve the technical issues with greater ease.

Interpreting Body Signals

Our body's tactile sensory system actively monitors everything we do physically. It receives and transmits signals that guide us throughout the day, and even at night while we sleep.

Although novice musicians may not have a private teacher to guide them, everyone, in my view has *inner teachers*, and without our "inner teachers" we couldn't learn to play a musical instrument. Our sense of hearing and our bodily tactile sense are the main sensory channels we use for playing music.

When we first begin playing guitar we are virtually flooded with physical sensations. Becoming adept at interpreting the signals our body sends us is an often overlooked tool. Professional musicians, without exception, have a vast inner sense of what the body signals mean and how to utilize them in the service of their playing.

Fortunately, there is a wonderful correlation between beautifully produced sounds and the physical actions that make them. In short, it feels good to play well. And, if you are fortunate, it feels great to play great!

Listening to Your Body's Signals

Learn to monitor and correctly interpret your body's signals. Allow your body to help guide you to mastery of the guitar. The build-up of tension, soreness, or aches of various kinds does not mean that you should "try harder." Once you have received the body's signal of discomfort, it means to rest for a moment, relax, and begin to look into the causes of the tension. Relaxation before repetition is better than constant repetition.

Backache

If you develop a backache, check the following:

1. Height of the foot stool. Try adjusting the height and seek a level which is more comfortable.

2. Keep your lower back straight. Slumping and bad posture increase lower back stress substantially.

3. Sit nearer the edge of the chair and lean slightly forward, with your feet positioned so that you feel well grounded as you begin to play.

4. Breathe fully, rather than shallowly. When you do not inhale fully your back muscles cannot relax as much as they need to. Over time the muscles will tire and begin to get sore.

Shoulder Ache

1. This is usually the result of sitting awkwardly, so review the steps for sitting position, and see if that helps.

2. If your shoulders are hunched when you play, let them return to their natural orientation.

Left or Right Forearm Tension

1. This results from inefficient leverage and too much muscular effort, in both left and right arm actions. Review arm and hand positions in order to create better leverage as you play.

2. Try a passage that you associate with an increasing level of tension, but reduce the pressure you are using to press the strings down. Ultimately, using the least amount of pressure and minimal muscular tension will help you increase the control of your playing. That in itself will reduce forearm tension.

Left Wrist Tension

1. Check the wrist and, if it is excessively bent, straighten it slightly.

2. Check the position of the thumb. It should be perpendicular to the neck of the guitar and be placed behind the first and second fingers. Study the section on left hand position and its accompanying photos.

Right Wrist Tension

1. If your wrist is straight when you play tension will tend to increase over time. It should be moderately bent as you play.

2. Make certain that your forearm rests gently on the shoulder of the guitar. If you press down too much on the guitar all the muscles will eventually tighten as a result.

Sore Fingertips

Sore fingertips are a very common occurrance for novices. Usually all soreness will disappear after a few weeks of moderate practice.

If soreness persists:

1. Your guitar may be at fault. The string action may be too high, or the frets may need adjustment. Have someone who is qualified look at your guitar to make sure it is not in need of repair or adjustment.

2. Novices almost always press too hard at first. Lighten your touch and practice using minimal left hand pressure. If you watch experienced guitarists play it seems as if they are barely pressing the strings down. That is an accurate observation. So experiment until you find just the necessary but sufficient amount of force to use for pressing the notes down.

3. For a while practice for shorter time periods and increase the resting time betweeen sessions.

Your body's signals, once you learn to interpret them, provide you with an infallible potential pathway for developing your mastery of the guitar. They are always true reflections of what you are doing, and there is almost nothing more fulfilling than resolving an ache, tension or pain into a cohesive set of actions that in turn produce beautiful musical sounds.

Chapter 8
Notes in the 1st Position

This chapter introduces you to the notes in the "first position" - that is, the notes in the first four frets of the guitar. Doing these exercises with consistent attention will greatly speed up your knowledge of the fingerboard.

Natural Scale

The natural scale simply means notes without either sharps or flats. The notes below are shown with their names, the string where they are located, and the fret they are played on. For this exercise use the left hand finger that corresponds to the fret. For example, the note F on the 6th string is played in the first fret using the first finger of the left hand.

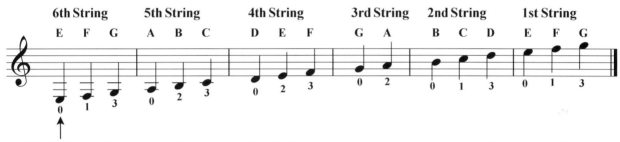

The "0" (see the notation above) is used to indicate that the note is played on an "open string."
"Open" means that the string is played without placing a left hand finger on one of the frets.

Exercise

Play each note 4 times. Use the natural scale written above as a guide. Play this repeatedly until you can easily name, locate and play each of these notes.

Chromatic Scale

The chromatic scale is a scale of consecutive 1/2 steps that uses both sharps (#) and flats (b) to indicate the fret the note is played in. Play and name each note 4 times.

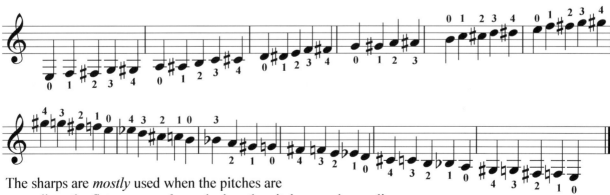

The sharps are *mostly* used when the pitches are ascending; the flats are *mostly* used when the pitches are descending.

Exercises on the 1st and 2nd Strings

1. Study the notes and their location on each string. Use the tablature notation below the staff to verify the correct fret to play on.

2. Without your guitar: look at each note and say aloud:
    a. its name
    b. its string location
    c. its fret location
For example: "F - 1st string, 1st fret; C - 2nd string, 1st fret."

3. With your guitar: play the notes of each exercise until you know them easily from memory.

Exercise on the 1st String

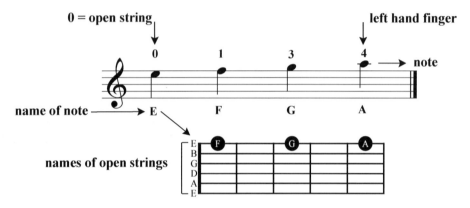

The 1st string plays mostly melody notes.   The note A on the 5th fret is included in this exercise. Just reach and stretch enough from your 1st position location when you need to play this note.

Exercise on the 2nd String

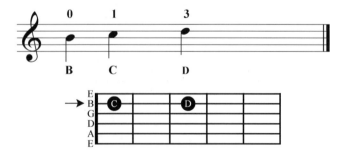

Notes on the 2nd string are also mostly used for melody.

Exercises on the 3rd and 4th Strings

Exercise on the 3rd String

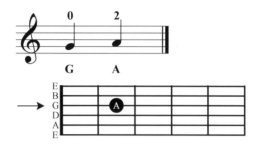

Notes on the 3rd string are very versatile. Usually they are middle voice parts, but they can also be melody or bass on occasion.

Exercise on the 4th String

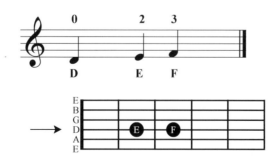

As a generalization, the notes on the 4th string are mostly bass notes.

Exercises on the 5th and 6th Strings

Exercise on the 5th String

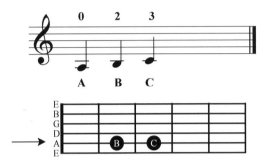

Notes on the 5th string are almost always bass notes.

Exercise on the 6th String

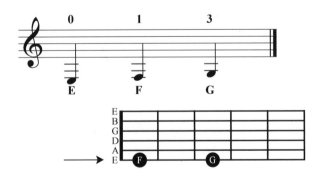

Notes on the 6th string are almost always bass notes.

Chapter 9

Right Hand Technique

The right hand is used to create sound by plucking and strumming the strings. The left hand, in a sense, just prepares the strings to be plucked. So it is the right hand that sets into vibratory motion the notes that the left hand has prepared for sounding.

Because each hand has a completely different role, that of preparation and that of "inputting" the sound, each has its own special techniques for mastery. ﹑

Right Arm Position

1. While sitting, and having adjusted the height of the footstool to a comfortable position, support the guitar by using your left hand to hold the neck of the guitar. Let your right arm rest at your side.

2. Now bring your arm up to a position where your forearm is resting on the upper shoulder of the guitar.

3. Keeping your wrist relaxed,
orient your fingertips towards the strings,
making adjustments until the fingertips are
touching the strings. The thumb is extended
across the rosette and is above the sound hole,
with i, m and a arrayed over and behind the rosette, a
little towards the bridge. The illustration here shown
has the thumb on the A string, with i, m and a
ready to pluck the notes of a chord on the upper three
strings.

Consider this to be a kind of *basic* position,
since, when you are playing, the right hand will *vary*
its touch point along the strings, either playing closer
to the bridge, for a brighter tone, or else playing a bit
more over the sound hole, for a darker, more mellow
tone quality.

4. When playing several notes successively on the
same string, the knuckles of the hand adjust to be
parallel to the line of the string being played. This
way, i and m, or another pair of fingers, can alternate
easily. Keep in mind that it is crucial that your
hand *feel* natural and comfortable during the
alternating of finger pairs.

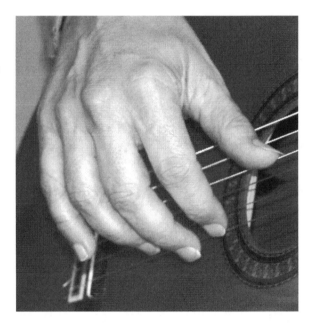

The sound will also tell you if the position is
working well: if the sound is even and smooth,
probably you have found a good position; if the
sound is uneven in amplitude, and it is hard to keep
a smooth rhythm, continue to adjust your hand and
finger posture until you are satisfied with the results.

5. When plucking the strings, the finger tip contacts the string at the left side of the finger, at the
junction between the nail and the flesh. There is a vast palette of tonal color available just within
the posibilities of using the nail, the flesh, and a combination of nail and flesh.

For now, focus on the basic position of the arm and hand, and begin to explore the sensations and
resulting sounds as you play the guitar. When your hand feels tight or fatigued, rest for a moment,
drop your hand to your side, and only when you are ready, return to your practice of right hand
technique.

Basic Techniques of Right Hand Fingering

Depending on the musical texture you are playing, the right hand has several types of finger actions available to it to create the musical effect you wish. The two most basic actions are called *free stroke* and *rest stroke*, and are described below.

1. **Free Stroke** (also called *Tirando*) consists of plucking a string with the fingertip, which then lifts slightly in its follow-through to avoid striking other strings.

2. **Rest Stroke** (also called *Apoyando*) consists of plucking a string with the fingertip, then allowing its follow-through to rest against the next lower-sounding string. When the thumb does a rest stroke, it will, of course, *rest* on the next higher-sounding string.

There is a lively debate among guitarists, that actually goes back to at least the 19th century, about when and how to use rest strokes and free strokes, and about whether to use flesh or nails.

My own opinion in these matters is quite simple. That is, learn to use *all resources of your right hand,* and be able to apply them in any manner you wish, according to the musical demand as you see it. Some will insist that all melody notes should be played using rest stroke. Some accomplished guitarists have even argued that rest strokes should never be used.

After all the dust settles, why not consider allowing the music to communicate to you exactly how each note may be plucked? Master musicians of other instruments have often chronicled their lifelong quest to find the best fingerings and articulations for the music they play.

3. **Alternating Fingers**, whether using free or rest strokes, is the most basic rule of right hand technique for playing melodies, scales, and single note patterns of all kinds. Alternation of i and m is akin to walking.

4. The thumb may, however, be used repeatedly.

Basic Principles of Right Hand Fingering

 Since most guitar music does not have much indication of which right hand fingering to use, it is crucial to learn the basic logic of right hand finger actions:

1. The thumb, with few exceptions, plays all the bass melody notes. In chords the thumb plays the lowest-sounding note.

2. The index and middle fingers, and, at times, the ring finger, play the notes of melodies and scales, using an alternating pattern as described above.

3. For arpeggios (that is, notes of a chord played one at a time) the thumb plays the bass note, and the index, middle and ring fingers cover the remaining notes on successive strings.

The right hand exercises on the following pages can be helpful in beginning to establish reliable patterns of finger alternation.

Exercises for the Right Hand Alone

All the exercises for the right hand in this section are played on open strings. This allows your full attention to focus on the position of your right hand and the actions of each finger. Begin slowly, then increase the tempo as you become more familiar with each pattern. Each of the exercises focuses on the underlying right hand technique for the playing of scales, arpeggios, tremolo, and chords.

Single Note Patterns

Exercises 1 & 2 are used when playing scales. At first practice using free strokes, then with rest strokes.

For exercises 1 and 2, practice alternating two-finger patterns of: i & m, then m & a, then i & a.

Keep your wrist gently bent. The use of the thumb should not disturb the actions of i, m & a.

Exercise 3 is a descending arpeggio pattern. Exercise 4 is an ascending arpeggio pattern.

Below is a tremolo pattern. Tremolo consists of rapidly repeated notes with a varied bass note pattern.

Be vigilant in the study of how the thumb works with i, m & a. Ideally they all work together smoothly.

Whereas the single note patterns apply to scale, melody and arpeggio passages, the two note patterns are reflections of harmonic and contrapuntal textures: that is, passages of two-note chords and two melodies played at the same time.

Two-Note Patterns

Gently, without tension, keep your wrist still. It should not wobble.

Some patterns will be easier than others. Over time the awkward patterns become easy and familiar.

At first play this very slowly. Then experiment with increasing the tempo.

Keep your thumb extended enough to avoid collisions with i & m.

Three and four-note patterns are simply the chords and harmonic progressions we find in all styles of music. The right hand fingering choices are inherently limited: in almost all cases the thumb plays the lowest bass note of the chord. Then i, m and a align to the other notes of the chord that lie above the bass note. If there are five or six notes in a chord we most often strum the chord using the thumb.

Three and Four-Note Patterns

Notes in chords should sound all at once. Keep your fingers close together to achieve this.

Exercises 14 and 15 are common accompaniment patterns used in many different styles of music.

The exercise below combines 4-note chords with arpeggios of those same chord notes.

This is a more varied pattern and it requires a deeper attention to play accurately.

Chapter 10

Left Hand Technique

Left Hand Position

In the illustrations below you can observe a front view of the left arm and hand, and also a view of how the thumb is positioned in the back of the neck of the guitar:

Notice how, in the illustration above on the left, the elbow is gathered in towards the body. This helps support the fourth finger as it extends to play the bass note of the GM7 chord being held.

And notice how, in the illustration above and on the right, the elbow is held away from the body, in order to allow the fingers to align to play the B7 chord.

Key Points about Left Hand Position

1. The wrist is slightly bent. If the wrist is too straight the fingers cannot reach all the notes. If the wrist is too bent, it becomes very uncomfortable, and your hand will tire quickly.

2. The thumb is perpendicular to the neck, approximately opposite the first and second fingers.

3. The fingers are curved to allow the fingertips to contact the strings and have efficient leverage to press down the string.

4. Allow a space of about two fingers' width between the neck of the guitar and the inside of your hand.

5. Most of the time the elbow is oriented slightly away from the side of the body. But, like the bowing arm of a violinist, the elbow adjusts by moving away from and close to the body depending on the technical requirements of the passage you are playing.

Finger Action

1. The fingers are curved and flexed to bring the fingertips to the strings.

2. The fingertips are placed just behind the fret of each note to be played. This prevents buzzes and produces a good tone.

3. Use minimal, but sufficient pressure when pressing down the strings. This conserves energy and allows the transition from note to note to be smoother.

4. Keep the fingers close to the strings before playing, in a curved shape, and use minimal lift-off when releasing a note. This increases the accuracy of your playing.

Basic Principles of Left Hand Fingering

Guitarists devote much of their musical lives to working out left hand fingerings that are musically sound and technically sensible. Each kind of musical structure, whether it is chords, scales, or arpeggios, has tricks of the trade that, once learned, can be applied again and again. The details of these approaches to fingering are covered in the exercises that follow. A brief outline of the main principles of left hand fingering is summarized below:

1. **One finger, one fret.** For any position you are playing in, the left hand fingers are placed in adjacent frets, whenever possible. For example, if the first finger is playing the F in the first fret of the E string, the F# in the second fret will be played with the second finger.

2. **Holding fingers down.** When changing chords, if both chords share a common note, the finger holding the common note is held down, while the other fingers move to the other notes of the second chord. This principle is explored and illustrated in detail in the chapters on chords and basic chord progressions.

3. **Sliding along a string**. When changing position, up or down the fingerboard, it is often possible to slide a finger holding a note to a note in the new position. Most of the time the sliding is done without creating a sound, with the string effectively guiding the fingers to the next location where the music is played.

Left Hand Exercises

Slurs

A *slur* is a curved line that connects two or more notes. It indicates that they are to be joined smoothly together. On the guitar this is done by plucking the first note of the slur in the normal way, then the left hand, *without* using the right hand, either *hammers-on* or *pulls-off* the remaining notes of the slur.   The slur can be applied to any combination of ascending and descending notes. The example below shows various kinds of slurs:

Ascending Slur, also called Hammer-on

To play the ascending slur, pluck the first note of the slur in the normal manner, then *hammer* the indicated left hand finger down just behind the fret of the second note.   The hammer action should be more like a light *tapping* than an action with great force or wild motion.

At first it helps to watch the finger that is tapping: guide it to a precise position just behind the fret of the second note. Keep the finger more curved than straight, and try to contact the string with the tip of your finger. A clear sound emerges when these elements are well integrated.

If the sound is not clear it means that the placement and curvature of the finger need further adjustment. Merely increasing the force of the movement does not usually improve the sound.

In the exercises below play each slurred pair 4 times. Rest the hand before continuing to the next pair.

Descending Slur, also called Pull-off

To play the descending slur, pre-place both notes of the slurred pair. Pluck the first note in the normal manner. Then *pull-off* the finger that is holding the first note so that the second note is sounded by the action of the finger that has pulled away from the string.

The left hand "pulling-off" finger is, in effect, *plucking* the string, in a way analogous to the right hand. It is also important that the finger holding the second note of the pair continues to exert enough pressure so that the action of the pull-off does not disturb it.

It takes focused practice for the slurs to attain reliable quality. You can measure the quality by listening to both the plucked initial note and the slurred note that follows. Over time the slurred notes will sound smooth and musically well-joined.

In the exercises below play each slurred pair 4 times. Relax the hand before practicing the next pair.

Pluck   The left hand pulls-off of the first note to sound this second note.

Slur exercises are one of the surest ways to develop finesse and fine muscle control of the left hand. Slurs develop control of the small muscles within the hand called the *interossei*. Spend a few minutes doing these exercises during each practice session. But do not over-work your hand.

It is better to rest briefly *as soon as* your hand begins to tire. Like the delicate gears of an old-fashioned Swiss clock, the interossei work for you automatically beneath the threshhold of conscious control.

That is partly why the pull-off and hammer-on techniques take special patience to master. Even so, once you have understood and practiced the essential elements, slurs become easy to do whenever required.

Two Note Intervals: Medieval Melodies in 3rds, 5ths, 6ths and Octaves

Medieval composers were the creative innovators who first began to harmonize single line melodies, in what the historians call "organum." Parallel organum means that the primary melody is accompanied note for note with another melody at a chosen *interval** - usually fourths, fifths or octaves. Below are four ancient melodies harmonized with intervals of thirds, fifths, sixths and octaves.

(*The term "interval" means the musical distance between two notes.)

Hymn to St. Magnus

Thirds: Thirds <u>always</u> are written from line to line or space to space within the staff.

Ambrosian Hymn

Fifths: Fifths <u>always</u> are written from line to line or space to space with one line or space between notes.

Begin to recognize the appearance and characteristic sound of the two note intervals in this section. Knowledge of the appearance and sound of intervals is a useful step towards the long term ideal of being able to imagine the sound just by looking at the musical score.

Song of the Donkey

Sixths: Sixths <u>always</u> are written from line to space or space to line with one and a half spaces between notes.

12TH CENTURY

Ballade

Octaves: Octaves <u>always</u> are written from line to space or space to line with two and a half spaces between notes.

RICHARD COEUR-DE-LION
(1157-1199)

Chapter 11

Guitar Chords

This chapter introduces you to the most basic guitar chords and shows you how chords are diagrammed.

How Chords are Diagrammed

Compare the photograph, on the right, of the Dm chord, with its chord diagram on the left. Once you understand the graphics, a chord diagram is easy to work with. Chord diagrams are, with occasional small variants, uniform in how they are presented, regardless of the guitar style you are exploring.

Over time, memorize the name and fingering placement for each chord you encounter. Also most of the basic chords have alternative fingerings. In the example below, sometimes it is better technically to use the 4th finger on the 2nd string instead of the 3rd finger. The musicwill usually suggest which fingering is preferred.

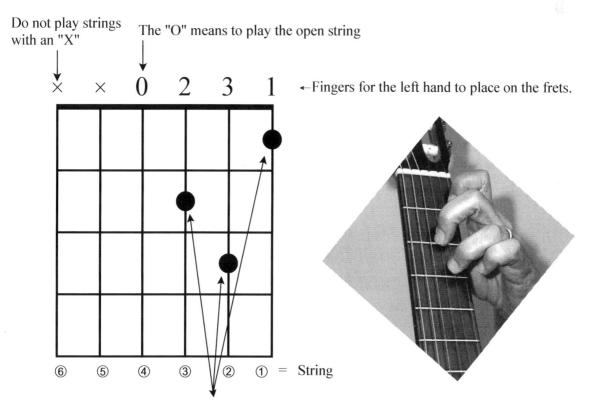

D minor = Chord Name

Do not play strings with an "X"

The "O" means to play the open string

←Fingers for the left hand to place on the frets.

⑥   ⑤   ④   ③   ②   ① = String

Where to place left hand fingers

Notes of the D minor chord

Hints on Playing Chords

1. <u>Memorize</u> all basic guitar chords. (In this section the chord diagrams will show the finger number *on* the fretboard. Most of the time fingerings are shown at the top line of the diagram.)

2. <u>Place down all fingers simultaneously</u>. At first this is elusive. Over time it will become much easier.

3. Study and practice the most efficient way of shifting from chord to chord:

    a. <u>Holding Down</u>: If two chords share one or more notes leave the "shared" finger(s) down. In other words, the "shared" note and finger stays in place while moving the other fingers to their new position. The chord diagrams below illustrate this important principle:

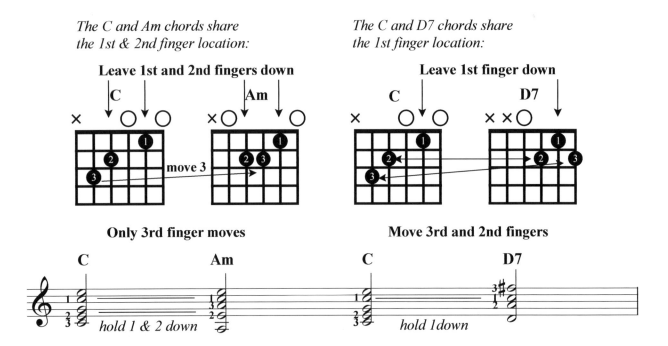

The C and Am chords share the 1st & 2nd finger location:

The C and D7 chords share the 1st finger location:

    b. <u>Slide a finger</u> along the string to the correct fret of the chord you are going to:

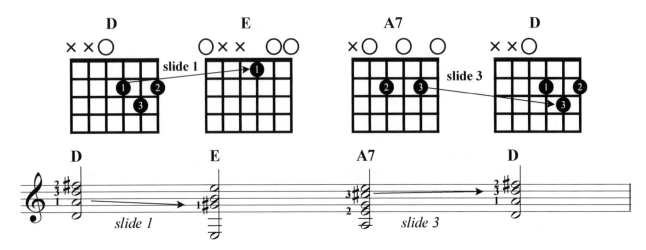

15 Basic Guitar Chords

In this section there are 15 chords which are essential for playing the guitar in any style.

To Play Chords:

Each chord is presented in music notation with its chord chart graphically presented above the notes.

Each diagram shows the correct placement of the fingers.

Remember that an "X" means don't play that string and that an "O" means to play that string open.

Above each diagram is the name of the chord. For example *Am* means A minor, *A* means A major, *A7* means "A dominant 7". Chapter 15 explores how chords are constructed.

Below the diagram are the notes sounded when you play the chord.

Once your left hand is holding down the strings, try strumming the chord notes with your right thumb.

Listen to and compare the sonic character of each kind of chord: major, minor, and dominant 7th.

For example, the A major chord, just by changing the 3rd string note from the note A to the note G, becomes transformed to A7.

Also compare the A chord to the A minor: A major becomes A minor by lowering the C# of the A chord by one fret to play a C natural. Each chord has a unique sound quality, and these different qualities are crucial to the inner workings of music structures.

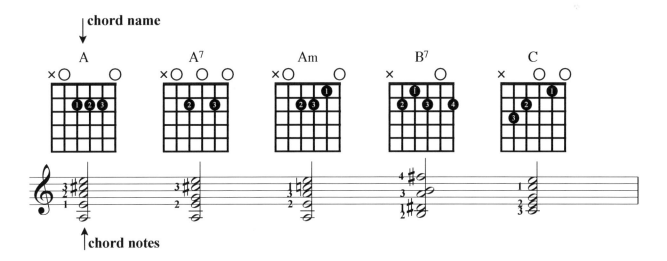

Remember that *everyone* learns chords *one* at a time. Then they are practiced in sequences called harmonic progressions. Each new chord takes about 6 weeks of introduction, practice, and review for it to start to become thoroughly familiar.

Keep in mind that chords by *themselves* are not meaningful *harmonically*. In order for chords to have musical meaning they are combined together in sequences called chord progressions.

Building up a basic vocabulary of chords is one of the most rewarding experiences for the guitarist. Just remember to be patient. There is no reason to be in a hurry. Each chord contains many dimensions of sound quality, so take time to experiment, play, and enjoy the character and challenges offered by each chord.

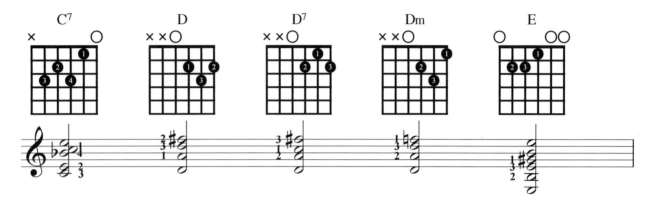

As mentioned, all of these chords occur in a wide range of guitar styles. The diagrams are excellent for helping you form a mental image of the layout of fingers on the fretboard.

The F major chord requires a 6 string bar. Look over the chapter on "Bar Chords" before learning this chord.

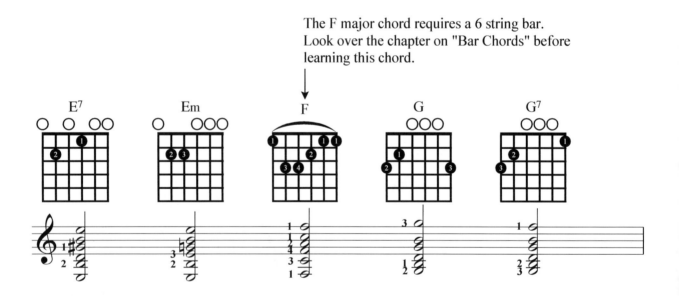

One goal is to be able to look at the chord's notes and instantly picture the fingering of the chord you are looking at. It may seem like a difficult task at first, but these chords recur so often that they eventually become completely familiar - in sound, visual appearance, and how they are fingered. Over time the reading and playing of chords becomes second nature.

Bar Chords

One finger of the left hand pressing down two or more strings simultaneously is called a bar. Barring is more difficult in the beginning stages of playing guitar than many of the other basic techniques.

The following is an explanation of the notation for bars, the different kinds of bars, as well as some hints on mastering the bar technique.

Bar Notation

The bar is notated with a simple group of symbols that give instructions about the bar.

What you need to know is:

1. The letter "**B**" above the notes to be barred indicates that a bar is to be used there.
2. A roman numeral (for example: **II**) tells you at what fret to place the bar.
3. The subscript number in front of the "B"→ ₃BII indicates how many strings are included in the bar.
4. A bracket indicates how long to hold the bar. If the bar is only for one chord there is no bracket.

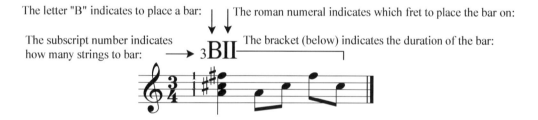

The letter "B" indicates to place a bar: | The roman numeral indicates which fret to place the bar on:

The subscript number indicates how many strings to bar: → ₃BII The bracket (below) indicates the duration of the bar:

There are several different kinds of bar. The most common are:

1. The **Full Bar** is when one finger covers all six strings:

BIII

Altlhough the illustration may give an impression that the bar finger is on top of the fret, it is actually positioned *just behind* the fret. Note that the bar finger is parallel to the fret.

2. When the bar finger presses fewer than 6 strings that is called a **Partial Bar**, or **Half Bar**. The term *half bar* lacks precision: in some editions it can refer to anywhere from 2 to 5 strings to be barred. For that reason I prefer to use the term *Partial Bar*. The subscript notation placed just before the bar indicator "B" will always tell you how many strings to bar. If the edition of your music lacks a symbol for how many strings to bar, it is easy to tell how many strings to bar by checking the note locations of the chord.

The **Partial Bar** can be done in two ways:

a. With a *straight* finger:

The tip of the bar finger, with just a little bit of pressure, can easily give the lowest note of the bar a full clear tone.

b. With the *finger bent* at the first joint:

In the photograph you can clearly see a gentle bend in the first joint of the bar finger. Not everyone's finger is capable of bending in this way. So if your index finger does not naturally bend do not worry about it at all. A two-string bar is the easiest of all the bar chord forms and a straight first joint works just fine.

Hints on Improving the Bar

At first playing bar chords is challenging. Novices try to use maximum strength and press as hard as possible to produce a clear sound. In reality it is leverage and properly engineered left hand placement that is most important.

Just about everyone, at first, tends to overwork the hand in the quest to get a good sound from the bar chord. Because tired muscles lack the necessary coordination for a successful result, practice the bar chords for a few minutes only, and learn to take a short rest as soon as you notice fatigue. A telltale sign of overworking the hand is when you feel an aching sensation in the muscles between the left hand thumb and the forefinger.

Be sure to rest your hand when fatigue sets in. There is no benefit in working at bar technique when your hand feels tired or stressed.

Keep in mind the following hints as you explore the bar:

   1. Keep the bar finger straight and absolutely parallel to the fret.

   2. Keep the bar finger close to the fret, just behind it. If you place the finger over the fret you will hear a muted instead of a clear sound. (In the photographs illustrating various bars, it *looks* as if the 1st finger is covering the fret. Actually the bar pressure is being fully applied *just behind* the fret. If your bar finger straddles the fret you will hear a muted sound. Keep making small adjustments until the sound is clear and without muting or buzzing.)

   3. Check the position of your left thumb - good placement will improve the leverage needed for a proper sounding bar chord.

   4. Apply only a reasonable amount of force when barring. More often than not, poor results when barring come from *lack of leverage* rather than lack of strength.

   5. So, if you hear a kind of muted-buzzy sound emerging from your attempts, do not assume you have applied insufficient force. Rather, see if you are already pressing too hard.

   6. It is more effective to completely restructure your hand position in the bar than to try to correct the bar while continuing to hold on to what is not working.

   7. Bar technique is best delved into *after* you have established a pretty good knowledge of the basic chords. Once you are comfortable with those chords (see pages 45-46 for the 15 Basic Chords) your technique will have grown to the point where a focus on bar chords will be fruitful.

Chapter 12
Common Chord Progressions

The 3 and 4-note chords of these exercises occur countless times in music of all styles. The four-note chords of each progression repeat the corresponding 3-note chord with a bass note added to fill out the harmony.

Each line of music contains three of the most common chords for the key indicated. Notice that the fingerings for the same chord often differ: the fingerings are determined not only by the notes of the chord, but also by the chord that comes both before and after. For example, whenever the same note belongs to two successive chords, we try to have the same finger play that note. Use the chord diagrams as a guide, both for finding the chord initially and also to create an inner visual picture of how the notes of the chord lay out on the guitar fingerboard.

C Major:

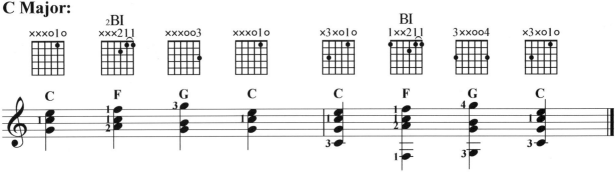

A 2-string bar is used to play the 3-note F chord.　　　　Use a 6-string bar to play the F chord.

A minor:

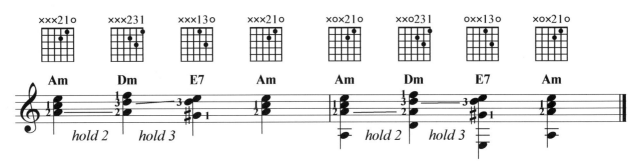

Hold the 2nd finger down when changing from Am to Dm; hold the 3rd finger down between Dm & E7.

G Major:

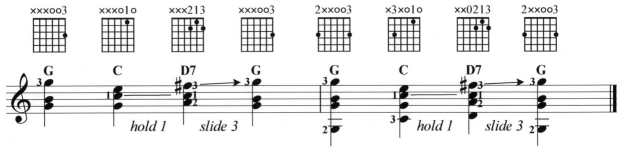

Try sliding the 3rd finger of D7 to the G chord.

50

Beginning students of guitar rightly wonder how to best build up their playing skills.
Just by learning these chords and progressions, and being able to recognize the visual
and sound quality of each chord, over a 3-9 month period, with careful attention and practice,
you can gain an excellent initial grasp of chord progressions on the guitar.

This page contains chord progressions of great significance because guitar composers
in all styles have favored the use of the keys of E minor, D major and A major for their compositions.

E minor:

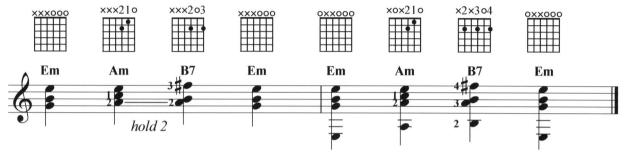

The second finger of the Am chord is held down while you move to the B7 chord.

D Major:

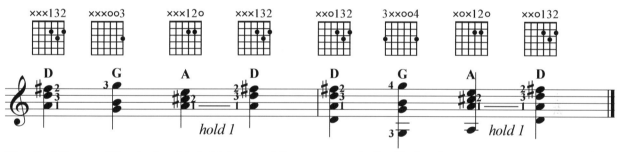

The first finger of the A chord is held down while you move to the D chord.

A Major:

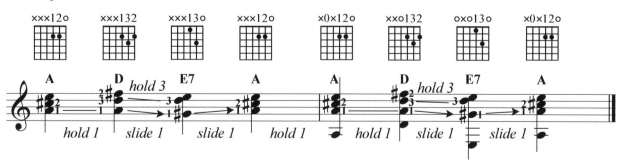

The first finger can be held down and slid back and forth from the note A to the note G#. Keep the 1st
finger down without lifting it off for the whole exercise. The first finger of the A chord is held down while
you move to the D chord. And the 1st finger also slides between the E7 and A chords.

The techniques of:

    a. <u>holding notes down</u> that are common to two successive chords,
    b. <u>sliding a finger</u> along a string to connect to a note of the next chord
    c. and <u>barring</u>

are fundamental to guitar mastery in every style. Your time and attention will be well rewarded as you learn all the chords individually by name and finger pattern, and then practice moving from one to the other in the harmonic patterns shown on these pages.

E Major:

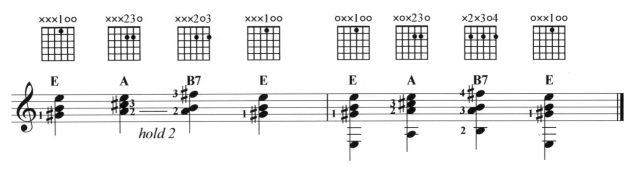

F Major:

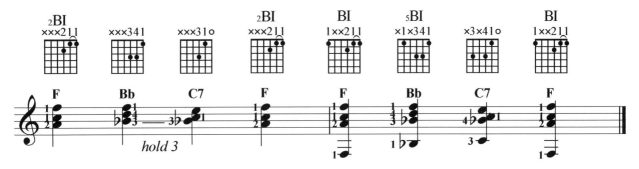

A 2-string bar is used to play the 3-note F chord.   Both the F & the Bb chord require a bar.

D minor:

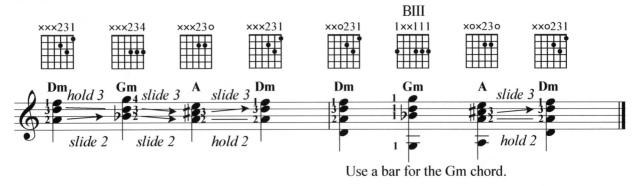

Use a bar for the Gm chord.

Notice how the 2nd finger can both slide and hold its place as you move from chord to chord.

Chapter 13
Basic Rhythm Exercises

When I tell my students that learning how to interpret rhythm notation is *slippery*, this is what I mean: on the one hand, everything we do, we do with rhythm. It is innate to our physical expression as human beings. The coordinative miracle of just walking across a room is beyond science to fully comprehend. Over many years I have met just a few people who were insensitive to melody or harmony. And virtually *everyone* can easily tap a rhythm in time to a beat.

Yet most adults, regardless of education or profession, have a tough time learning to play the rhythmic structures of music. It may seem paradoxical, but I believe that our innate musicality actually tends to get in the way. We can usually make a pretty good *guess* as to how long a note should be played. And, even if the guess is not correct, as long as the pitch content is accurate, the ear doesn't necessarily make us stop for a correction. This is because *rhythm is extremely flexible and can manifest in many ways.* Almost everyone immediately detects a wrong pitch or chord, even on the first hearing of a piece. Wrong rhythms are more elusive to recognize.

If you have a teacher, he or she will guide you. Another alternative is to use a computer music notation program like Sibelius or Finale. These programs have an abundance of educational materials and can greatly assist you in your exploration of rhythm notation.

With or without a teacher, you can now begin by practicing these basic rhythm exercises in two ways:

1. Without your guitar, tap and count aloud each rhythmic pattern.
2. With your guitar, play each pattern, while counting mentally as you play.

Whole Notes and Whole Rests

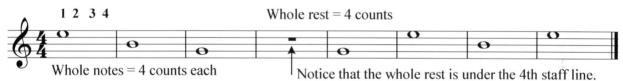

Whole rest = 4 counts

Whole notes = 4 counts each

Notice that the whole rest is under the 4th staff line.

Half Notes and Half Rests

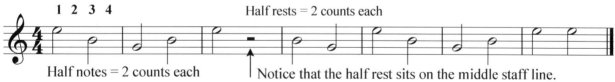

Half rests = 2 counts each

Half notes = 2 counts each

Notice that the half rest sits on the middle staff line.

Quarter Notes and Quarter Rests

Quarter Notes = 1 count each

Quarter rests = 1 count each

Dotted Half Notes

Dotted half notes = 3 counts each

Eighth Notes and Eighth Rests

Notice that 2 eighth notes equal the time value of 1 quarter note.

The exercise below explores the notation of dotted notes and tied notes. Dotted notes extend the value of the note before the dot by one half the value of the note they modify. Tied notes extend the value of the note they are tied to by the value of the note itself.

Dotted Quarter and Tied Quarter Notes

In the example above, compare the continuous eighth notes in the second staff with the dotted quarter notes in the staff above. A dotted quarter note equals 3 eighth notes.

The examples and exercises below briefly explore notations for sixteenth notes and rests and also dotted eighth notes.

Sixteenth Notes and Sixteenth Rests

Dotted Eighth Notes

Compare the continuous sixteenth notes notated in the second staff with the dotted eighth notes above. Notice that a dotted eighth note equals 3 sixteenth notes.

Remember to be patient when working on rhythm notation. A solid mastery of rhythm is developed over time as you work on a broad range of music that employs a wide diversity of rhythmic structures.

Rhythm Exercises in Two Voices

Classical guitar music is often composed with two or more voices. (In two-voice music the upper voice is usually the melody, while the lower voice is the bass.) Novices are often puzzled by the task of understanding and playing multiple voices notated on the same staff. The exercises below are all written in two voices and exclusively with open string sounds. The upper voice is written with the note stems pointing upwards, and the lower voice has the note stems pointing down.

Before playing these exercises, try tapping them: left hand, bass; right hand, melody.
Learn them separately and then try them together. When playing use the R.H. thumb for all bass notes; use i, m or a for the melody notes.

4/4 Time

3/4 Time

Just about everyone *already has* a good sense of rhythm, but only those intent on mastering music notation become easily fluent in reading rhythmic structures. This page of exercises contains other common time signatures, and also dotted 8th notes, 16ths, and triplet 8th note passages. They can guide you into a deeper clarity about the elements of rhythmic notation and how they are organized.

With patience, and determination, you will gain mastery of 2-part rhythm structures.

2/4 Time

6/8 Time

The 6/8 time signature receives 6 eighth note counts per bar:

Rhythm Words

The oldest known complete piece of music comes from ancient Greece and is dated to around the 1st century AD. It is carved into a tombstone and known as the *Seikilos Song*, Above the text of the inscription are symbols for the musical notes of the song. Since at this time there was evidently no notation for rhythm, the *words* themselves are the only clues to what the rhythms of the song were. (See page 84 for a guitar arrangement of *Seikilos Song*.)

Today we can use "Rhythm Words" to facilitate understanding of various rhythms. They are helpful for getting a "feel" of how rhythms sound in combination with one another. Although they don't replace an accurate counting of rhythms, they can help clarify *how* rhythms of short passages of music go together.

Use the chart below to make an association between a rhythmic value, for example a 1/4 note, and its rhythm word, which is the word *Play*. (For example: ♩ = Play; ♫ = Steam-boat).

Rhythm Word & Corresponding Rhythm

Short Examples

Chapter 14 How Scales are Constructed

The term *scale* refers to the tonal material of music arranged in an order of rising pitches. Scales are the building blocks of music. Think of them as a kind of musical DNA. Everything in music - from melody, to chords, to harmonic progressions, is related to the scale that the music is in.

We have previously explored music notation, both for pitch and rhythm. Now we are in a position to take another step. To take this step we return to the concept of musical intervals.

Intervals

An interval is the musical distance between two notes.

Half-Step

The 1/2 step is the smallest interval. On the guitar a 1/2 step is formed between any two notes on adjacent frets of a string. Also, a 1/2 step is formed between any open string and the first fret of that string. In the example below the notes F# & G are on adjacent frets and form a 1/2 step interval:

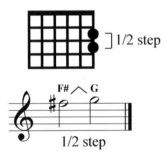

Whole Step

A whole step is equal to two 1/2 steps. On the guitar a whole step is formed between any two notes that are two frets apart. In the example below the notes F and G of the first string are a whole step apart:

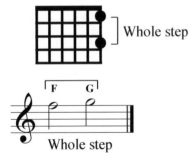

The Intervals Used to Construct Scales

All scales are built out of 1/2 steps and whole steps. The sequence and placement of the 1/2 and whole steps determine the *kind* of scale being played. The three most important kinds of scales are called *major*, *minor* and *chromatic*. Major and minor scales are called *diatonic* scales, which means the scale has seven tones. The chromatic scale uses all twelve notes within an octave.

Major Scales

The major scale is a diatonic, or seven tone, scale. It consists of five whole step intervals and two 1/2 step intervals. The 1/2 step intervals always occur between the 3rd & 4th tones, and the 7th & 8th tones of the scale. Illustrated below is a major scale built beginning on the note C. The note C is called the *tonic*. Tonic means the first and main note of a scale.

In the C major scale written below study the notes, the placement of the 1/2 and whole step intervals, and listen carefully to the character of the major scale as you play it.

Scale of C major:

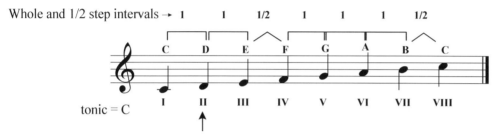

In music theory roman numerals are used to number each note of a scale.

Minor Scales

There are three kinds of minor scales. They are called *natural*, *harmonic* and *melodic* minor. The first five tones of all minor scales have the same sequence of 1/2 and whole tone intervals. Each of the three kinds of minor scale has different intervals between the sixth and seventh tones.

Natural Minor

The natural minor is a diatonic scale. The 1/2 step intervals are placed between the 2nd and 3rd tones, and the 5th and 6th tones of the scale. The other five intervals of the scale are whole steps.

In the natural minor scale written below, with a tonic of the note A, study the notes, the placement of the 1/2 and whole step intervals, and listen carefully to the character of the natural minor scale as you play it.

Scale of A natural minor:

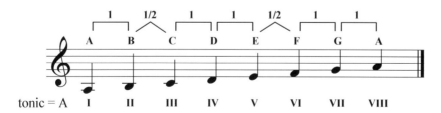

Harmonic Minor Scale

The first six notes of the harmonic minor are the *same* as the natural minor scale.
The interval between the sixth and seventh notes of the scale is called an *augmented second*.
The augmented second has three 1/2 steps between the two adjacent scale notes. In the example below the three 1/2 steps are between the note F and the note G#.

The harmonic minor scale imparts a distinctive flavor and is often used in flamenco music.

In the harmonic minor scale written below, with a tonic of the note A, study the notes, the placement of the 1/2 steps, whole step and especially the augmented second interval. Listen carefully to the character of the harmonic minor scale as you play it.

Scale of A harmonic minor:

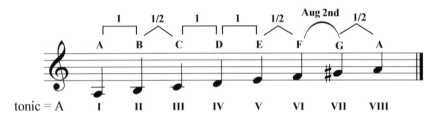

Melodic Minor Scale

The melodic minor scale combines the qualities of both the natural and harmonic minor scales. By learning the melodic minor scale, in various keys, you will also be practicing the complete *set* of notes found in the natural and harmonic minor scales.

The first five notes of the melodic minor are the same as the natural and harmonic minor scales. It is the variations of the sixth and seventh notes that impart its distinctive character. Notice that the sixth and seventh notes vary, depending on whether the scale is ascending or descending. In the ascending scale the sixth and seventh notes are each raised by 1/2 step, and in the descending scale the sixth and seventh notes are lowered by 1/2 step.

In the A melodic minor scale written below study the notes and the placement of the 1/2 and whole steps. Listen carefully to the ascending and descending scale as you play it.

Scale of A melodic minor:

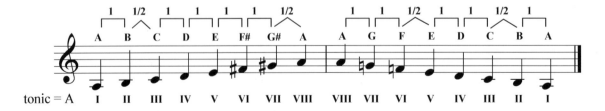

Throughout this book the melodic minor scale is emphasized. Later on in your studies you may wish to work with the natural and harmonic minor scales in greater detail.

Chromatic Scale

The chromatic scale consists entirely of 1/2 steps. Unlike the diatonic major and minor scales, it has twelve notes, and uses every tone within a span of one octave.

Sharps are used when ascending, and flats are used when descending. The chromatic scale is excellent as an exercise to develop technique on the guitar. Within the music you play there may be occasional small segments that use a chromatic scale.

In the chromatic scale written below, based on the note E, study the notes and the sequence of the 1/2 steps, both ascending and descending. Listen carefully to the "uniform" sound of the chromatic scale as you play it.

Chromatic scale beginning on the note E:

A Few More Thoughts About Scales

Keep the following essential elements in mind as you study scales:

    1. Work on only one scale at a time.

    2. Write out the notes of the scale. Visualize where the notes are played on the guitar and listen intently to the succession of whole and 1/2 steps.

    3. Memorize the scale.

    4. After a few weeks the smoothness and tone quality will get better and better. Don't be in a hurry. And refine your intention, as necessary, to play each scale with complete accuracy. When you make an error, take a breath and begin it again, repeating with care and patience until it sounds the way you wish.

    5. When the left hand is consistently playing the correct sequence of notes, try using different pairs of right hand fingerings.

        a. Begin with i & m alternating.
        b. Then use m & a until that combination feels more natural.
        c. Then also experiment with i & a.
        d. Practice all the scales until both free strokes and rest strokes can be applied at will.

    6. The exercises and preview pages for each key contain more detailed practice scenarios and suggestions for you to explore when you are ready.

Major and Melodic Minor Scales
in the first and second positions

This page presents the scales of the nine major and minor keys that are most commonly used for guitar. Study and play these scales until they are completely familiar.

Chapter 15
How Chords are Constructed

Chord

A chord is three or more notes sounded at the same time. Chords are the building blocks for the harmonic design of music. Each chord has its own distinctive sound and structure. In this chapter we will define and explore the most common chords.

Triad

The music theory term for chord is *triad*. A triad is a chord of three notes. There are four basic triads. They are called *major, minor, diminished* and *augmented*. Each kind of triad has a distinctive sound that comes from the individual structure of the triad itself.

Interval Structure of Triads

Traids are built using *minor* and *major thirds*. These two kinds of thirds are combined in various ways to create the vast harmonic palette of our musical language.

Minor Third

A minor third is defined as a whole step + a half-step. It is abbreviated using a lower case "m" followed by a 3:

$$m3 = \text{minor third}$$

For example, the interval formed by the notes A + C is a minor third. In the previous section on how scales are built, we learned that the interval from A→B is a whole step, and the interval from B→C is a half-step.

When the notes A and C are played together they sound a minor third:

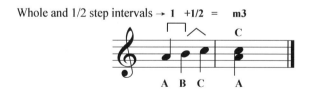

By playing and looking at the scale notes of A, B and C in the example above, you can begin to decipher the character of the minor third interval, with its internal interval structure of a whole step + 1/2 step.

As long as the *harmonic* interval between the two notes is a minor 3rd, it does not matter what the *sequence* is of the whole and 1/2 step sequence *within* the minor 3rd.

Major Third

A major third is defined as a whole step + a whole step. It is abbreviated using an upper case "M" followed by a 3:

M3 = Major third

The interval of the notes A + C# is a Major third.

When the notes A and C# are played together they sound a Major third:

Play and listen to the notes above. By playing and looking at the scale notes of A, B and C#, you can learn to recognize the sound quality of the Major third interval.

Major Chords

A major chord is a triad that is built as follows:

Major 3rd (M3) + minor 3rd (m3)

For example, a major triad built on the note C, consists of the notes C, E and G:

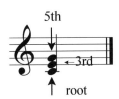

The lowest note C is called the *root*. The middle note E is called the *3rd*. The note G is called the *5th* of the triad.

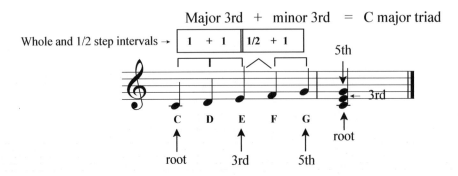

The root, 3rd and 5th are all notes of the C major scale, numbered by their position in the scale, starting with the note C.

Minor Chords

A minor chord is a triad that is built as follows:

minor 3rd (m3) + Major 3rd (M3)

For example, a minor triad built on the note C, consists of the notes C, Eb and G:

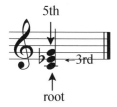

The lowest note C is called the root. The middle note Eb is called the 3rd. The note G is called the 5th of the triad.

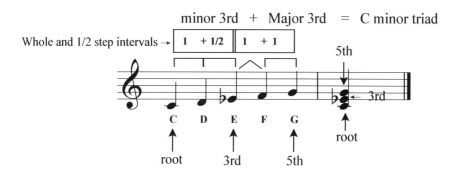

The root, 3rd and 5th are all notes of the C minor scale, numbered by their position in the scale starting with the note C.

The major and minor triads comprise the vast majority of chords in the music we play.   We have seen that their structure is:

Major triad = M3 + m3

minor triad = m3 + M3

Diminished and Augmented Chords

There are only two other possible triadic structures. They are as follows:

diminished triad = m3 + m3 (abbr: *dim.*)   Augmented triad = M3 + M3 (abbr: *Aug.*)

Illustrated above is a B diminished triad.   Illustrated above is a C augmented triad.

Chapter 16
Why Musicians Study Keys

A question often asked by beginning guitarists is "What do you mean when you say a piece is in a major or minor key? And what use is it to know about keys?"

This is a bigger question than it first appears. As an example, let us look into the key of C major. Johnny Cash, Wolfgang Amadeus Mozart and Duke Ellington all composed music in the key of C Major. Over hundreds of years countless compositions in C major have been written and played. So despite easily hearable differences in style, what are the main elements of musical structure that all pieces in the key of C Major share in common?

To answer this question let us now look at the fundamental structural elements of the key of C Major.

The Scale of C Major

The universally shared common ground among pieces in C Major is the scale from which the music is derived. Here are the notes of the C Major scale written in one octave:

When you play these notes you will of course intuitively recognize the quality of the scale. These are the white keys of a piano keyboard and the natural notes of all other instruments, including the guitar.

Now let's begin to explore the complete set of notes on the guitar that comprise the C Major scale. The lower range (shown below) is found on the 6th and 5th strings. The 4th, 3rd and 2nd strings contain the middle range. The upper range is mostly found on the 1st string. (We stop for convenience at the 12th fret of the 1st string, but the notes of the C scale continue up to the final fret of the fingerboard.)

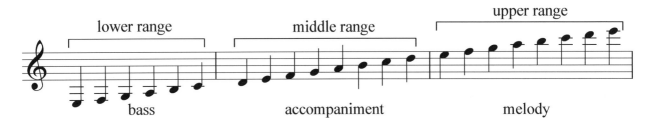

As a general guide the lower range is where most bass notes are placed, the middle range includes bass, accompaniment and melody notes, and the upper range is mostly used for melody notes.

The Chords of C Major

Returning to our initial scale of one octave, we will now use the notes of the scale to build the chords most commonly used in the key of C Major:

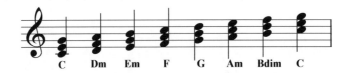

It is not immediately necessary, but if you wish to review the chapter on how chords are built, that may serve as a refresher as to how and why the chord notes above are generated.

For now just keep in mind <u>that the 7 notes of a C major scale are used to create melody</u>. <u>Also the same 7 notes are used to build the set of chords that naturally belong to the key</u>.

During the first years of my own study of the guitar I always had the feeling that the *next* note or chord could be *any note or any chord found on any part of the fingerboard*.

Although that feeling was not completely wrong, I just did not have any useful concept of how notes of a piece of music were organized. In fact any "next" note has a very high probability of belonging to the scale itself. And any "next" chord will probably belong to the set of chords natural to the key.

The 7 notes of the scale are in essence a kind of DNA from which all the music in that key is created. It is easy to deduce that a knowledge of the scale itself is a way to greatly advance your playing.

Trained professional musicians seemingly make music effortlessly, but it is not just by talent alone. Part of their mastery is because they have understood concepts of musical structure that vastly simplify musical actions. Music for the novice is truly a complicated and often confusing enterprize. Developing as a musician can be thought of as a gradual transformation of the complicated into the simple. This process is available to everyone. This is because music, like language, has an intrinsic structure and our minds are capable of observing and applying the elements of structure to our musical activities.

Even so, musical concepts, while valuable in themselves, need to be cultivated in the mind of each player, along with patience, a sense of adventure and a serious intent to develop musical understanding.

But for now let us limit our exploration to the two most important chords that comprise the harmonic structure of the key of C Major.

Two Chords

The two chords are written below:

C Major   G Major

Why these two chords? To explore the answer let's introduce three terms of music theory. They will be useful for continuing this discussion and also for later in your studies.

1. **Root**. The term "root" means the note that generates a chord. The root is the note that gives any chord its name. So in our current discussion the note C is the *root* of the C major chord.

2. **Tonic**. The term "tonic" means the first and main note of the scale or key. Tonic also refers to the chord built on the first note of the scale. So in our discussion, the note C is the tonic of the key of C major, and the C major chord is the tonic chord of the key of C.

3. **Dominant**. The word "dominant" refers to both the *note* and the *chord* that is built on the fifth note of the scale. In our discussion the note G is the fifth note of the C scale and is called the dominant.

Students often ask: "Why do I need to bother with theory? I just want to play music on my guitar." Well, in truth you can skip these concepts and immediately get going as best as you can.

This is possible, in my opinion, because everyone's musical mind already knows a vast amount about music. Musical knowledge is embedded in intuition and functions on your behalf at all times.

Perhaps the essential point is that a trained musician and a novice process music notation very differently. Of course everyone sees the same staff, notes, rhythms, etc. Look at the example below:

Novice View

The novice guitar player looks at the first note, names it, checks which string and fret it is played on, figures out which fingering to use, then plays it. Proceeding one note at a time, as if stringing pearls on a necklace, the novice is limited to this repetitive exercise until he, by intuition, or by conscious application, deepens his approach.

So how does the trained musician see differently than the novice?

The trained musician sees and organizes the sequences of notes into musical blocks and at a glance sees the key, the scale, the chords and the overall musical design. This is done by having learned basic concepts and applying them to the score. Once you begin integrating these basic concepts you will no longer read music as an endless chain of notes, but rather according to how the music is organized.

The trained musician sees the notes and groups them something like the example below:

Trained View

C chord arpeggio   C scale descending   C chord arpeggio G chord arpeggio C chord

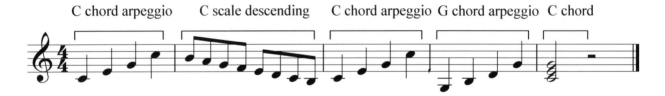

Instead of 23 separate notes, begin to see how notes can be grouped according to musical design: scales, chords and arpeggios are universal design elements. Each of the 5 segments bracketed above is either a scale, chord or arpeggio. Use this example as a model for your own study of the music you play. Play each segment separately until you can play all notes within each group as a single unit.

There is nothing miraculous or inaccessible about this. It is merely a matter of intent, emphasis and follow through. Just as painters observe and enjoy the play of light in nature and art, we musicians enjoy and savor the infinite display of musical patterns that manifest out of the primary elements of scale, chord and arpeggio.

As you listen to the music, observe how your musical imagination responds to these elements of musical structure. You can thereby initiate a lifelong adventure of discovery and enjoyment.

C Major in the 1st Position

To review, here is the basic information we have discussed so far:

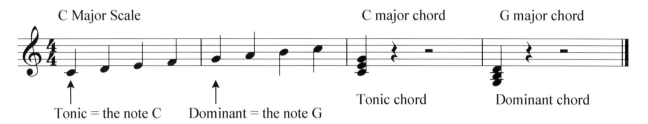

Tonic = the note C   Dominant = the note G

As a practical application, let us now write out all of the notes of the C and G chords that are found in the first position of the guitar:

Observing that the note G occurs in both the C and G chords, there are 12 notes that span the 1st position and they are the most prevalent notes found in pieces written in C major for the guitar. Using only notes of the tonic C and G chords above, study the second half of Fernando Sor's Etude in C Major, Opus 60, #1:

FERNANDO SOR

The two Fs and the A notated below are the *only* notes <u>not</u> part of either a C or G chord.

Notice that both Fs and the A are part of the C scale. When you are ready, go to the page 92 and play the whole etude of Sor. Whenever you play any piece in the key of C major you can refer to these illustrations and models. If you wish to, make a careful study and try to find all the scale, chord and arpeggio segments that you now are familiar with. See where the composer places the tonic C and the dominant G in the composition.

Don't expect, however, that everything is going to fit *exactly* into these models. If that were so the music would rapidly become boring.

For now, whenever you play a piece in C major, study how the composer uses tonic and dominant chords as a structural device.

Chapter 17

Three Special Techniques

There are a few "special effects" techniques that greatly add to the palette of sounds a guitarist can use. It is not difficult to learn these techniques. Our arrangement of *Sakura, Sakura* on page 113 uses the techniques of harmonics, pizzicato and tambour.

Natural Harmonics

Natural harmonics are high bell-like sounds that are produced while lightly touching a string at what is called a "node". The term *node* means an exact fractional point along the length of a string. Natural harmonics are *not* hard to play, although a few minutes of help from a teacher, or friend who plays guitar, can save a lot of time and unravel the initial mystery that we encounter as we delve into this technique.

The illustration shows the left hand finger touching the harmonic node at the 12th fret of the first string:

On the guitar the three nodes most frequently used to create natural harmonics are at the string's:

   12th fret = which is the 1/2 way point,
    7th fret = which is the 1/3 way point, and
    5th fret = which is the 1/4 way point.

To play a natural harmonic:

1. Place the indicated finger of the left hand to touch, not press down, the string just *above* the fret. (If you are touching either before or after the fret the tone will be unclear.)

2. The right hand plucks the string in the normal fashion. Usually use free strokes for this effect.

3. When you are touching the exact location of the node on the string, the harmonic sound literally blooms with a beautiful bell-like purity.

The notation to indicate harmonics sometimes varies from one music edition to another, but here below is the most common way to indicate the harmonic notes and where to play them:

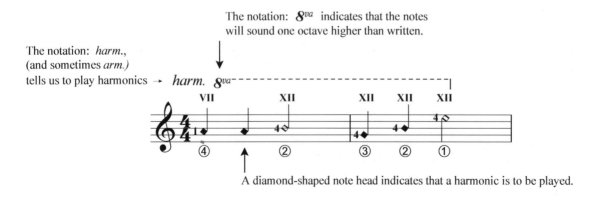

The notation: *8va* indicates that the notes will sound one octave higher than written.

The notation: *harm.,* (and sometimes *arm.*) tells us to play harmonics →

A diamond-shaped note head indicates that a harmonic is to be played.

Pizzicato

Pizzacato is only occasionally used on guitar. (It is more familiar in the violin family of instruments, when the bow is put down and the player plucks the strings with the fingers of his bowing hand.)

On the guitar the effect is made by placing the heel of the right hand just over the bone of the bridge. Then the thumb plucks the strings to make the effect. Also sometimes known as *étouffé*, which means muted, it can be found is several works of Fernando Sor. Like harmonics, it can be a bit baffling at first, but in a short time becomes easy to play.

When starting to play pizzicato the right hand thumb is extended so it can contact the strings. In pizzicato the hand placement is the most important element. After a few minutes of experimentation you may notice muffled drum-like sounds emerging from your guitar. That means you are on the right track. The illustration below shows the right hand preparing to play pizzicato:

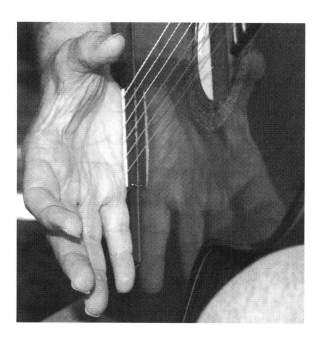

Pizzicato Notation

Pizzicato is notated with a dot above the note. The abbreviation *pizz.* is also usually included for clarity.

The dot above or below the notehead indicates that it is played pizzicato.

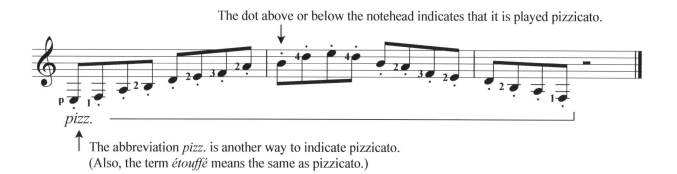

The abbreviation *pizz.* is another way to indicate pizzicato.
(Also, the term *étouffé* means the same as pizzicato.)

Tambour

Tambour is a simple technique. When you see the notation *tamb.*, instead of plucking the notes in the normal way, you tap the side of your right hand thumb against the strings, as if you were playing a tambourine. One thing to to remember is to literally bounce the thumb on and off the strings. If the thumb rests on the strings after tapping there will be no sound. That is because the thumb, by resting on the strings, stops the strings from making any sound.

The illustration below shows the right hand thumb just as it is tapping down on the strings:

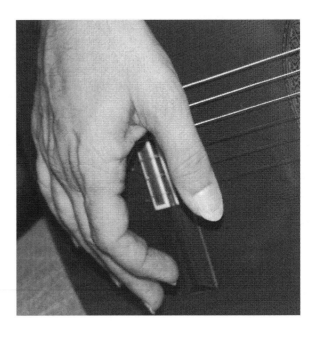

Try using the tambour technique on these two chords from *Sakura, Sakura* (on page 113)*:*

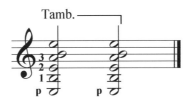

Chapter 18

Sight Reading

Playing at sight music you have never seen before is a skill and pleasure every guitarist can cultivate. By following the guidelines in this chapter, you can develop and improve your sight reading ability.

Many novice musicians forgo useful prepatory steps in this process. If you learn to do a few things *before* actually playing that will make the endeavor much more successful.

Before Playing

1. Check the key signature. Be sure you know which notes are sharp or flat throughout the piece. See if you can determine what key you are playing in. For example D major, or A minor.

2. Check the time signature. How many beats are there per bar? What kind of notes are to be counted? Usually you will count quarter notes (for example: 3/4 time) or eighth notes (for example: 6/8 time).

3. Also it is helpful to review the tempo markings (Allegro, Lento, etc.) Tempo reflects the character.

4. If there are accidentals within the piece that are not in the key signature, locate them on the fretboard.

5. Make sure you understand the rhythms and other musical symbols (such as repeats, harmonics etc.).

During Playing

1. Try not to get bogged down. Sight reading is more like a rough sketch than a finished painting. In the initial stages, just try to develop a sense of the overall character of the piece.

2. Play the melody line alone. Usually the note stems of the melody will be pointing upward.

3. Play the bass line alone. Usually the note stems will be pointing downward.

4. Look at each measure to determine if the musical design is primarily:

    a. Scale motion
    b. Arpeggio motion (notes of a chord, one at a time)
    c. Chordal (two or more notes played at the same time)

5. Now play the whole piece. Try to focus more on the music's overall shape than on all the details.

Scale Motion

If the passage is primarily scale motion, look for the beginning note, whether the scale rises or falls (its contour), and the ending note:

Chordal Passages

There in no easy way around the effort it takes to learn to read chords. This is because the eye tends to "bounce" from note to note. And, the more notes there are, the longer it takes to place the fingers for the chord. Single notes are easy to read. Vertical stacks of notes take longer to decipher.

But there is a way to organize your eye and hand. Over time, if you follow this method, you will learn to read chords much more quickly. Here outlined is a method that many guitarists find useful.

When sight reading chords:

1. First, locate the <u>highest</u> note of the chord and place it down. Usually this is the melody note.

2. Second, locate and place down the <u>lowest</u> note. This is the bass note and often gives the chord its name.

3. Once you have placed the melody and bass notes, fill in the interior notes between these boundaries.

Try the following examples, placing the chord notes down one at a time in the order indicated:

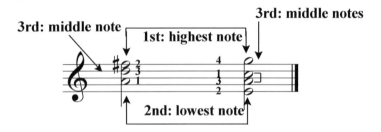

Arpeggio Motion

Arpeggios are notes of a chord, played one at a time. When you see an arpeggio, practice placing the fingers on the notes <u>all at once</u> in the chord shape that the arpeggio outlines:

Chord Shapes

Arpeggios of the Chord shapes above

Waltz

from <u>Complete Method for the Guitar</u>, Opus 59

Above each bar is an indication of the various musical elements Carcassi employs to create this Waltz.
Before playing, using the guidlines for sight reading, review the musical design of each bar. For the
bars marked with 3rds or octaves (abbr: 8ve) review the exercises on page 105 for the key of
A minor. See how skillfully Carcassi employs all these elements within the Waltz.

MATTEO CARCASSI
(1792-1853)

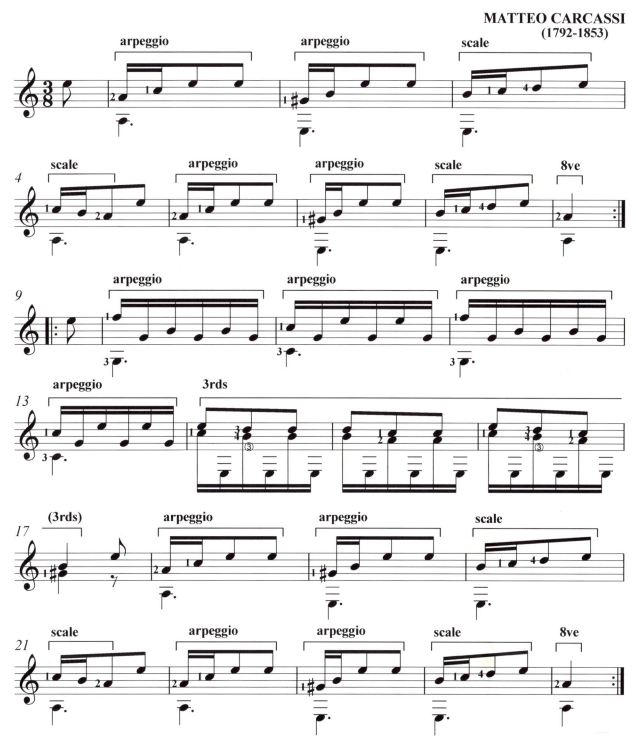

Sight Reading Repertoire

This section introduces you to reading music on the guitar. All of the melodies are short, and the selections are well-known creations of great classical composers. The first selection, *Jesu, Joy of Man's Desiring,* is in the key of G major. Review the G major scale, notated on page 115, then play the melody, which uses the notes of the G scale.

Except for the note G on the first string, the left hand fingerings are always the same as the fret that the note is played in. Check out the boxed letter a below. Use the 4th finger (instead of the 3rd finger) on the note G on the first string: this produces a much smoother melodic flow and is better than using the 3rd finger on the note D of the second string and immediately on the note G that follows.

Throughout this book all fingerings are chosen to provide a smooth transition from note to note or chord to chord. Good fingerings are always influenced by the flow of the music and not merely by the simple context of fret-to-finger the beginner may initially prefer.

After you learn to play the *Jesu, Joy of Man's Desiring* melody, you may wish to check out page 120, where you can play an arrangement of this melody with Bach's original bass line added.

Jesu, Joy of Man's Desiring
from Cantata # 147

JOHANN SEBASTIAN BACH
(1685-1750)

a   4th finger plays the note G in the 3rd fret.

This is a bit harder, but musically better.

Notice that the rhythmic structure of Bach's melody is entirely of quarter notes.
Each quarter note receives one count.

Menuett
from the Anna Magdalena Bach book

"I was obliged to work hard.
Whoever is equally industrious will suceed just as well." J.S. Bach

JOHANN SEBASTIAN BACH
(1685-1750)

Wachat Auf
from Six Schübler Chorales for Organ

JOHANN SEBASTIAN BACH
(1685-1750)

The Four Seasons

"If acute and rapid tones are evil, Vivaldi
has much of the sin to account for..." Charles Burney (1776)

Spring I

ANTONIO VIVALDI
(1675-1714)

Autumn I

ANTONIO VIVALDI
(1675-1714)

Winter II

ANTONIO VIVALDI
(1675-1714)

Eine Kleine Nachtmusik
from Serenade No. 13 for Strings, K. 525

"Mozart is sunshine." Antonin Dvořák

WOLFGANG AMADEUS MOZART
(1756-1791)

Turkish Rondo
from Piano sonata No. 11, K. 331

WOLFGANG AMADEUS MOZART
(1756-1791)

Symphony No. 9
Fourth movement, first theme

*"Prince, what you are, you are by the accident of birth; what I am
I am of myself. There are and will be thousands of princes.
There is only one Beethoven."* L. v. Beethoven - letter to Prince Lichnowsky

LUDWIG VAN BEETHOVEN
(1770-1827)

Symphony No 5
Fourth movement, first theme

LUDWIG VAN BEETHOVEN
(1770-1827)

Symphony No. 6
Third movement, first theme

LUDWIG VAN BEETHOVEN
(1770-1827)

Nutcracker Suite

"Music is not illusory, but revelation."
P.I. Tchaikovsky

March

PETER ILLYITCH TCHAIKOVSKY
(1840-1893)

Tempo di Marcia Viva

Waltz of the Flowers

PETER ILLYITCH TCHAIKOVSKY
(1840-1893)

Tempo di Valse

Dance of the Sugar Plum Fairy

PETER ILLYITCH TCHAIKOVSKY
(1840-1893)

Peer Gynt Suite No. 1

"The more deeply the heart is moved, the more reticent, the more enigmatic is the expression." E. Grieg

Anitra's Dance

EDVARD GRIEG
(1843-1907)

In the Hall of the Mountain King

EDVARD GRIEG
(1843-1907)

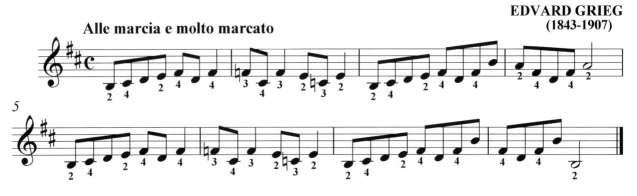

Morning Mood

EDVARD GRIEG
(1843-1907)

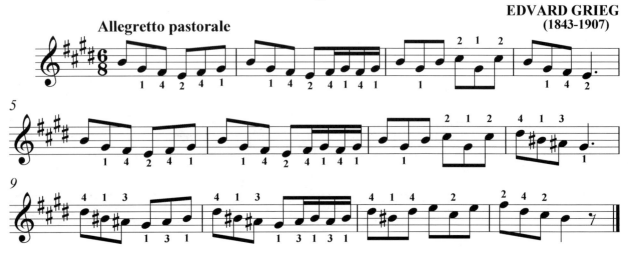

Pictures at an Exhibition

"I am a realist in the highest sense - that is, my business is to portray the soul of man in all its profundity." M. Mussorgsky

The Great Gate of Kiev

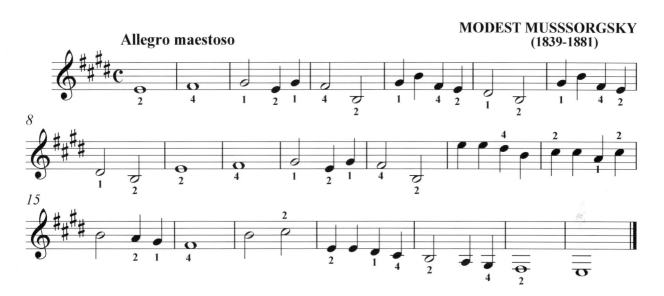

The Old Castle

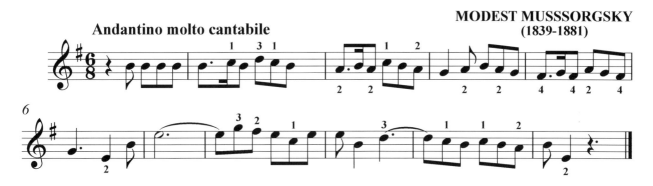

Promenade

Two Ancient Melodies

Music notation spans human culture for more than 3000 years. Here are two ancient melodies:

Hymn for the Emperor

The legendary founder of Chinese music was Ling Lun, who was famous for making bamboo pipes tuned to the sounds of birds. Music was seen as central to the harmony and well-being of the state. It is said imperial inspectors would visit the provinces to report on the condition and quality of the music of the local region.

ANCIENT CHINESE
(1000 B.C.)

Seikilos Song

The Seikilos epitaph is the oldest known complete musical composition. It was found engraved on a tombstone near Ephesus. It states: *"While you live, shine. Don't suffer anything at all; Life exists only a short while, And time demands its toll."*

ANCIENT GREEK
(1st Century A.D.)

PART TWO

Selected Repertoire

About this section

This section contains nine chapters of repertoire, with each chapter concentrating on a basic key the guitar plays in. The last chapter is dedicated to flamenco, with an introduction to elementary flamenco strumming, and includes three flamenco pieces.

It is organized in this sequence:

Chapter 19 - key of C major

Chapter 20 - key of A minor

Chapter 21 - key of G major

Chapter 22 - key of E minor

Chapter 23 - key of D major

Chapter 24 - key of A major

Chapter 25 - key of E major

Chapter 26 - key of F major

Chapter 27 - key of D minor

Chapter 28 - Flamenco

How to use this section

This section contains the music. It is organized according to the nine basic keys that the guitar plays in. It begins with a chapter for the key of C major, then is followed by chapters for each of the other major and minor keys. The C major chapter is followed by the chapter for A minor, then G major, and so on.

Each chapter has a structure:

    I. It begins with a Preview page that contains:

        1. the notes of the scale in one octave,

        2. the set of scale notes in the 1st and sometimes the 2nd positions,

        3, the tonic and dominant chords for the key.

    II. The next page contains eight short exercises tailored to the key itself:

        1. **Scale**. The notes of the scale, ascending and descending.

        2. **Melodic Thirds**. An exercise in melodic thirds. Practice this after you memorize the scale.

        3. **Chords**. A basic chord progression for the key. Play each chord and practice shifting from chord to chord until the movements feel familiar and require a minimum of effort.

        4. **Arpeggios.** This is an arpeggio pattern of the chord progression above. Learn to recognize the chord from which each arpeggio is derived.

        5. **Thirds**. This is a scale of thirds. Thirds are the building blocks for chords. A knowledge of how to play thirds within each key is a powerful tool for your musical and technical development.

        6. **Sixths**. The scale of sixths is a good exercise for developing the left hand position.

        7. **Octaves**. The scale of octaves helps you become familiar with the same note in different registers, for example the note C on the 5th string, and the note C an octave higher on the 2nd string.

        8. **Tenths**. The scale of tenths helps develop the *vertical* stretching capacity of the left hand.

Exercises 1-4 prepare you to play the repertoire for the chapter you are working in.
Exercises 5-8 may be added gradually over time. These exercises are useful for players at all levels.

Keep in mind that alternating between repertoire and exercises, over time, without expecting *instant* mastery, is both realistic and very fruitful. These exercises are so fundamental that musicians of all instruments utilize them over their lifetime for study and stimulus to their technique.

    III. The music for each chapter begins with a duet. The solo pieces that follow are organized with the easier coming first and more challenging pieces following. These are pieces that appeal to novices, yet are enjoyable to return to as the years go by and your skills advance. Works of Bach, Sanz, Mozart, Aguado, Sor and traditional flamenco are today as fresh and captivating as when they were first composed.

What is important about keys and why this knowledge is helpful

Each major and minor key has a definite set of musical and technical characteristics. As you begin to understand how keys and their chords function on the guitar, it organizes your knowledge and enhances the potential of your musical activities.

In general, keys that are <u>easier</u> to play have their main chords built on notes that are one of the three open bass strings. The major and minor keys of E, A and D (which are the *open* bass strings) have a rich abundance of music written in them.

Keys that are <u>harder</u> to play have main chords built on bass notes that are *not* open strings, and they often have chords and transitions that are relatively awkward to master.

F major is a more awkward key to play in

The key of F major is a good example of a key that is relatively hard to play in, both because the bass notes limit the scope of the composer's available melodic range, and because it is necessary to use bar chords for the tonic chord of the harmonic design.

The bar chord of F is awkward to play for novices: *The Ab is the highest melody note without too much stretching:*   *The dominant C major chord is not hard to play, but it also has a limited melodic range from the fifth string location up to the Bb:*

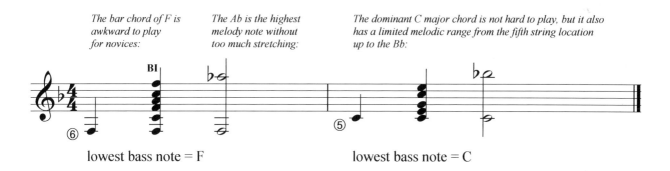

lowest bass note = F   lowest bass note = C

A major is an easier key to play in

Keys that are easier to play take full advantage of open bass strings for the main chords. The key of A major has the 5th string open for its tonic chord and the 6th string open for the dominant chord.

The A chord is easy to play and can be fingered in several ways to make easy transitions to other chords   *Using the open A bass note, the melody can be played anywhere.*   *The dominant E major chord is easy to play, and easy to transition to and from.*   *Using the open E bass note, the melody can be played anywhere.*

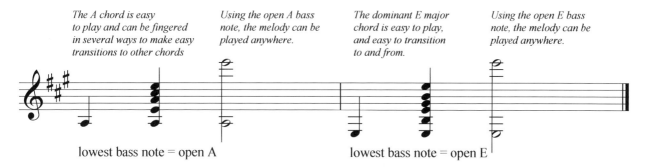

lowest bass note = open A   lowest bass note = open E

Over time you will learn to play in most any key, but the principles of how harmonic designs are translated to the guitar remain constant.

Chapter 19

Key of C major

This chapter introduces the key of C major.

It contains:

Preview of C major

Eight short exercises

A duet by Jean-Philippe Rameau

Solo repertoire by Sor, Carcassi, Roncalli, and Rameau

Arpeggio Patterns from Sor's <u>Method for the Spanish Guitar</u>

Preview of C major

The C major scale in one octave

Notated below is a one octave scale of the key of C *major*.

tonic*   dominant**

(* *Tonic* is the term for the <u>first</u> note and chord of a key.)
(** *Dominant* is the term for the <u>fifth</u> note and chord of a key.)

Notes of the C major scale in the 1st position

Tonic and dominant chords of the key of C major

The C major chord (notes = C, E, G) is the *tonic* chord built on the 1st tone of the C major scale.
The G major chord (notes = G, B, D) is the *dominant* chord built on the 5th tone of the C major scale.

Tonic chord = C major

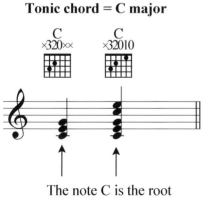

The note C is the root
of the C major chord.

Dominant chord = G major

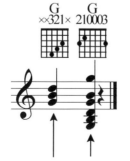

The note G is the root
of the G major chord.

(Keep in mind that the term *root* means
the note that generates the chord.
The *letter* name of any chord is *always*
the root of the chord.

Key of C major
8 short exercises

Minuet en Rondeau

Rameau was a contemporary of Bach and was a famous court composer of French opera.
This minuet comes from his *Pieces de clavecin* and is the first one of the collection.

JEAN-PHILIPPE RAMEAU
(1683-1764)

Etude

Opus 60 # 1

Sor composed this etude as a single line of melody notes, with only a few chords
to mark the end of phrases. Yet there *seems* to be a bass melody - this is cleverly
contrived by Sor by having some of the melody notes function as both upper melody
and lower bass at the same time. As you play this piece, see if you
can hear Sor's implied bass line.

FERNANDO SOR
(1778-1839)

Etude

In this very short etude Sor introduces just a hint of a true bass line.
Sor was always skillful and inventive in his translation of the 19th century
Mozartean style to the idiomatic nature of the guitar.

FERNANDO SOR
(1778-1839)

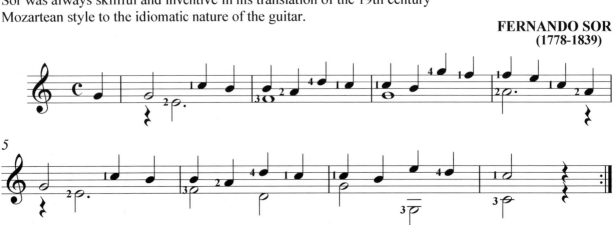

Prelude

from Complete Method for the Guitar, Opus 59

Carcassi wrote, *"I shall always esteem myself amply reworded for my labour, if I can obtain the certainty of having composed a useful work."*

MATTEO CARCASSI
(1792-1853)

Waltz

from Complete Method for the Guitar, Opus 59

MATTEO CARCASSI
(1792-1853)

D. C al Fine.

Minuet

Count Ludovico Roncalli was an Italian nobleman who published a set of suites for baroque guitar.

LUDOVICO RONCALLI
(1654-1713)

Ductia

The *ductia* is a rare medieval dance form. Note the two part counterpoint and the "hollow" sounding harmonies of 5ths and 8ves.

13TH CENTURY DANCE

Two Etudes
Opus 60 # VIII and IX

Etude VIII is a musical model that Sor uses to create Etude IX. Sor repeats the harmonic
design of VIII, but composes a new melody and a flowing accompaniment of 8th notes in Etude IX.
On the following page both etudes are presented in score form for further study and insight.

Etude VIII

FERNANDO SOR
(1778-1839)

Etude IX

FERNANDO SOR
(1778-1839)

Two Etudes in C major from Opus 60

Each of these etudes is notated separately on the previous page.
This is <u>not</u> a duet. Study how Sor composes a flowing variation in 8th note motion
out of the stately simple elements of Etude VIII. Try playing measure one of
Etude VIII and then play the corresponding first measure of Etude IX below. It is a rare
opportunity to study how a great 19th century master of the guitar approached composition.

FERNANDO SOR
(1778-1839)

Etude
Opus 35 # I

"He who wishes to follow me will find that the object of my theories is to teach
and persuade, since I establish nothing by authority. These are not
precepts which I give, but researches which I communicate."
F. Sor, Method for the Spanish Guitar, published in London in 1850.

FERNANDO SOR
(1778-1839)

Etude
Opus 35 # I

This is the same music as on the previous page. The tonic C and dominant G harmonic passages are bracketed and labeled below. The bracketed passages all have either the note C or the note G as the bass note. As you learn to look for the tonic C and dominant G notes within the bass regions of pieces in the key of C it is a good guess that the other notes of the same area will belong to those harmonies. (At times you will find exceptions: further harmonic study will clarify this.)

In time you can learn to recognize these harmonic patterns. Also keep in mind that the notes C and G <u>can</u> function in other ways than as the roots of the C and G chords. It reflects the genius of our musical language that the same note can function in many ways. But mostly they will function in their primary role as roots of the chords to which they give their name.

FERNANDO SOR
(1778-1839)

Etude
Opus 31 #1

Sor's Maxim # One: *"To regard the effect of the music more than
the praise as to skill as a performer."* from his <u>Method for the Spanish Guitar</u>.

Beginning at the measure marked with [a] there are three parts - melody, bass, and a simple middle part.
The middle part begins with a quarter rest sign: and is followed by the 3rd string quarter note "G".
The quarter note symbol at times has to be offset a bit horizontally so it does not collide with the other
pitches of the melody and bass parts. This offset does not effect the counting of the rhythm.

Although three-part writing at first may seem confusing, over time you will become comfortable with
this aspect of music notation, particularly if you keep in mind that each melodic strand - whether
there are one, two or three parts, is counted separately within each measure. The music of Bach,
Dowland and other baroque masters is commonly written in three parts.

FERNANDO SOR
(1778-1839)

Minuet en Rondeau

This is a solo version of the duet at the beginning of this chapter.

Once you have worked on the piece and it is familiar, you may wish to create some variety of *timbre*.
Timbre means tone quality or tone color.

To do this, try contrasting the right hand position during repeated sections:
play it once with the R. H. near the bridge, then on the repeat try bringing the R. H.
above the sound hole of your guitar.

JEAN-PHILIPPE RAMEAU
(1683-1764)

C Major Arpeggio Patterns
from Sor's <u>Method for the Spanish Guitar</u>

This set of arpeggio exercises comes from Sor's *Method for the Spanish Guitar*. The first line is a harmonic pattern from which all the arpeggio variations are derived. Sor, along with other 19th century masters, favored use of p, i and m of the right hand. The ring finger was used to play chords of four notes.

Be sure to become comfortable with the harmonic pattern first. Then go on to explore the various right hand arpeggios. Although they are challenging, they have much to offer.

Harmonic Pattern:

FERNANDO SOR
(1778-1839)

These exercises are excellent for right hand fingering patterns and for the harmonic progression Sor has written in the key of C major. Work on one or two at a time. After a while let them go. Then go back to the same exercises. Returning again and again to worthy music and technical exercises, after letting them go, is better than doggedly sticking to any one subject matter. You will find that a study pattern of concentrated effort followed by a release of focus produces better results than sheer determination without allowing the mind to rest and absorb.

Chapter 20

Key of A minor

This chapter introduces the key of A minor. A minor is called the *relative* minor of C major. The term "relative" means that both C major and A minor "share" the same key signature. Both C major and A minor have no sharps or flats within their key signatures.

This chapter contains:

        Preview of A melodic minor

        Eight short exercises

        A duet by Georg Friedrich Handel

        Solo repertoire by Albeniz, Aguado, and anonymous works such as Greensleeves, Packington's Pound, Brian Boru's March and Sakura.

Preview of A melodic minor

The A melodic minor scale in one octave

Notated below is a one octave scale of the key of A *melodic minor*. See the preceeding section on the structure of scales for a review of how the melodic minor scale is constructed.

See how the 6th and 7th notes of the scale vary in ascending or descending motion.

tonic*   dominant**

(*Tonic* is the term for the <u>first</u> and main note and chord of a key.)
(** *Dominant* is the term for the <u>fifth</u> note and chord of a key.)

In the key of A melodic minor the notes F and G are often varied. The note F can be raised to an F#, and the note G can be raised to a G#.

Composers can freely change *any* note at any time, in both major and minor keys. But, in general, minor keys have more pitch variation than major scales. And it is the 6th and 7th tones of the minor scale that most frequently are altered.

Notes of the A melodic minor scale in the 1st and 2nd positions

The notes F and G are "sharped" as the scale ascends, and lowered, using naturals, as the scale descends.

Tonic and dominant chords of the key of A minor

The A minor chord (notes = A, C, E) is the *tonic* chord built on the 1st tone of the A minor scale.

The E major chord (notes = E, G#, B) is the *dominant* chord built on the 5th tone of the A minor scale.

Tonic chord = A minor

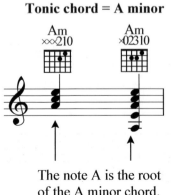

The note A is the root of the A minor chord.

Dominant chord = E major

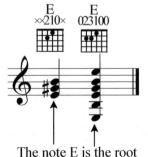

The note E is the root of the E chord.

(The term *root* means the note that generates the chord. The *letter* name of any chord is always the root of the chord. For example: Am → A is the root; Em → E is the root; D7 → D is the root.)

Key of A minor

8 short exercises

Scale

Melodic Thirds

Chords

Arpeggios

Thirds

Sixths

Octaves

Tenths

Minuet

In 1785 Charles Burney wrote, *"Handel's general look was somewhat heavy and sour; but when he did smile, it was his sire the sun, bursting out of a black cloud. There was a sudden flash of intelligence, wit, and good humour, beaming in his countenance, which I hardly saw in any other."*

GEORG FRIEDRICH HANDEL
(1685-1759)

Spanish Etude

based on Leyenda

Use R. H. thumb on all bass notes.

ISAAC ALBENIZ
(1860-1909)

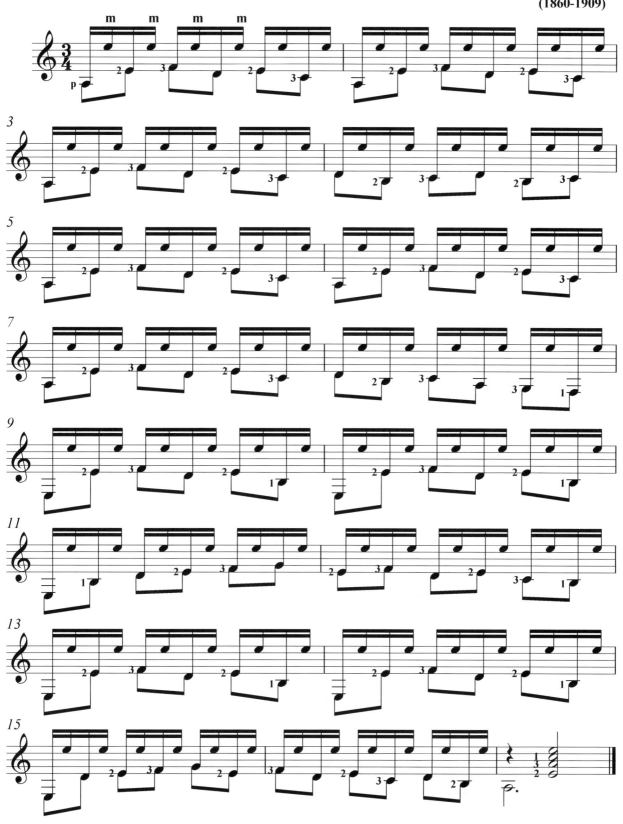

Two Hungarian Dances

I
Cifra Beszéd

Andantino

ANONYMOUS
(19th Century)

Fine

D.C. al FINE

II
Magyar Biharitól

Grazioso

ANONYMOUS
(19th Century)

Etude in A Minor
lesson #19 from *New Guitar Method*

Aguado composed this arpeggio study exactly as shown in the second staff. Every group of four notes of the arpeggio pattern can be condensed into the chord pattern that is shown in the first staff.
Practice placing the left hand fingers down in the chord shape above each arpeggio group.
Once you are very familiar with the chord progression, play the arpeggio study. Going back and forth between chords and arpeggios is an extremely good way to master arpeggios written in any style.

Observe how each chord is made up of the arpeggio pattern below:

DIONISIO AGUADO
(1784-1849)

Greensleeves

This late 16th century version of Greensleeves comes from William Ballet's Lute Book, which is in the library of Trinity College in Dublin, Ireland. Along with works of John Dowland, popular tunes and settings of songs mentioned in Shakespeare's plays, this setting of Greensleeves has a purity and simplicity of great appeal. The composer of the melody remains unknown.

Although almost everyone knows the tune, it is worth spending some time examining the recurring rhythmic patterns - the dotted 8th note followed by a 16th and an 8th is a rhythmic *motif:*

(see the bracketed element in measure one below) that lends character and elegance to the melody.

In music a *motif* is an element of the music - for example, a rhythm, or a short melodic fragment - that recurs throughout the music. This rhythmic motif is used 13 times in Greensleeves. Notice that the rhythmic motif is independent of the melodic content: the melody is constantly changing yet the rhythmic motif remains the same.

Packington's Pound

This piece is an natural musical companion to Greensleeves. Both were written originally for the lute. They share the same key of A minor and include beautiful excursions to the key of C major. Whichever piece you learn first, the second will seem easier and more familiar due to the shared elements of melody, harmonic design, and style.

ANONYMOUS
(16th Century)

Brian Boru's March

Brian Bóruma (c. 941-1014) was an Irish king who helped unify Ireland with successful military adventures characteristic of that time. It is often played by Irish harpists and the tune itself can be found in many arrangements. Our arrangement begins with a brief Adagio, with the march commencing at the Con Moto of line one. Con moto means "with movement." This section is to be played with a flowing faster tempo. Try ♩. = 80.

ANONYMOUS
(old Irish tune)

2nd time: play a little slower to the end

Sakura, Sakura

This iconic melody is often played by the Japanese koto. Using harmonics, pizzicato and tambour transform the guitar's sound palette to evoke the delicate atmosphere of this timeless melody. See Chapter 17 for an explanation of how to play these special techniques.

ANONYMOUS
Japanese folk song

Chapter 21

Key of G major

This chapter introduces the key of G major.

It contains:

Preview of G major

Eight short exercises

A duet by Joseph Bodin de Boismortier

Solo repertoire by Kuffner, Newsidler, Carulli, Bach, Carcassi, Sor and Aguado

Preview of G major

The G major scale in one octave

Notated below is a one octave scale of the key of G *major*. (See the preceeding section on the structure of scales for a review of how the major scale is constructed.)

tonic*   dominant**

(*_Tonic_ is the term for the <u>first</u> and main note and chord of a key.)
(** _Dominant_ is the term for the <u>fifth</u> note and chord of a key.)

Notes of the G major scale in the 1st position

Tonic and dominant chords of the key of G major

The G major chord (notes = G, B, D) is the *tonic* chord built on the 1st tone of the G major scale.
The D major chord (notes = D, F#, A) is the *dominant* chord built on the 5th tone of the G major scale.

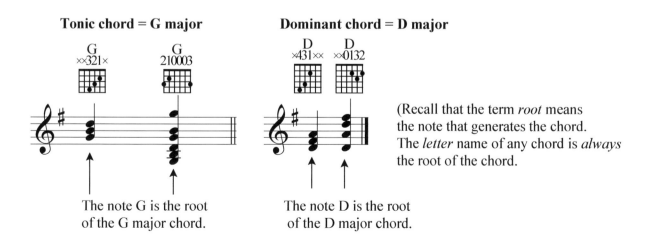

Tonic chord = G major

Dominant chord = D major

(Recall that the term *root* means the note that generates the chord. The *letter* name of any chord is *always* the root of the chord.

The note G is the root of the G major chord.

The note D is the root of the D major chord.

Key of G major
8 short exercises

Minuet

Boismortier was a French baroque composer of instrumental music, opera, ballets, and vocal music. He moved to Paris in 1724 and there became famous as an independent composer. He is notable historically because he was able to conduct his entire musical career without either the patronage of the nobility or employment by the church.

JOSEPH BODIN DE BOISMORTIER
(1689-1755)

Andantino

Küffner was a violinist with the Würzburg court orchestra,
and was a prolific composer of guitar music.

JOSEPH KUFFNER
(1776-1856)

Renaissance Dance

Newsidler was a German lutenist
who lived in Nürnberg and published eight books of tablatures.

HANS NEWSIDLER
(1508-1563)

The Girl I Left Behind Me

IRISH JIG

Lento

Carulli, born in Naples, Italy, began his musical studies on the cello,
but adopted the guitar as his instrument of choice. In 1808 he moved
to Paris, where he lived as virtuoso, composer and teacher until his death in 1841.

FERDINAND CARULLI
(1770-1841)

Jesu, Joy of Man's Desiring

from Cantata # 147

"I have always kept one end in view, namely, with all good will to conduct a well regulated church music to the honour of God." J. S. Bach in a letter to the Mühlhausen Council.

JOHANN SEBASTIAN BACH
(1685-1750)

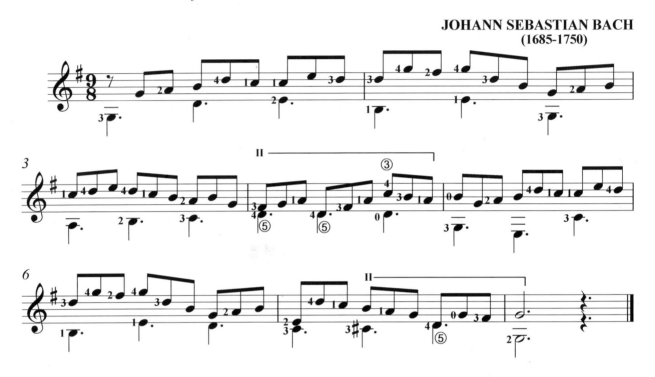

Prelude

from *Complete Method for the Guitar*, Opus 59

Look for the underlying chord shapes for each arpeggio group.

MATTEO CARCASSI
(1792-1853)

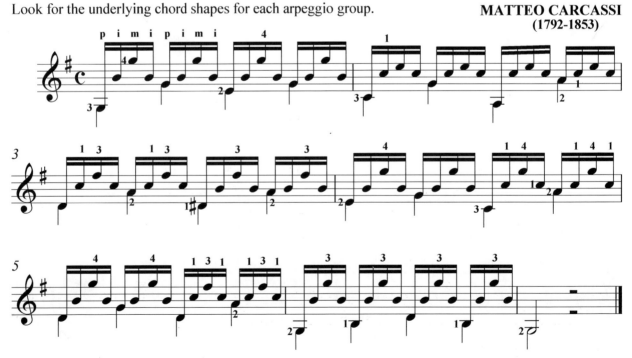

Waltz
Op 51 # 1

Sor's Maxim #6: *"Never to make any ostentation of difficulty in my playing, for by doing so, I should render difficult what is the least so."* from his <u>Method for the Spanish Guitar</u>.

FERNANDO SOR
(1778-1839)

Waltz

lesson #7 from _New Guitar Method_

Aguago writes, _"To my way of thinking, the guitar has its own particular nature: it is sweet, harmonious, melancholy; sometimes it can even be majestic, although it does not allow of the grandiosity of the harp or the piano."_

DIONISIO AGAUDO
(1784-1849)

Etude

lesson #15 from _New Guitar Method_

Aguado writes, _"Great care should be taken with the fingering of both hands."_

DIONISIO AGAUDO
(1784-1849)

A Toy
originally for lute

During the 17th century it was not uncommon for dinner guests of the aristocracy
to be invited to inscribe a piece of music into the family music book. Since public
printing was still the exception rather than the rule, these family music
books - originally intended for private use and enjoyment - are now priceless
archives of the music of that epoch.

JANE PICKERING'S LUTE BOOK
(17th Century)

Chapter 22

Key of E minor

This chapter introduces the key of E minor. E minor is one of the special keys that has a treasure trove of musical masterpieces that the guitar can play. Bach's Lute Suite #1, Villa Lobos' Preludes #1 and 4, transcriptions of Frescobaldi, Albeniz, and Granados are but a few of the pieces guitarists play in the key of E minor.

This chapter contains:

Preview of E melodic minor

Eight short exercises

A duet arrangement of Bach's Bourée from the 1st lute suite

Solo repertoire by Ravenscroft, De Visée, Carcassi, Sor, and Goodman

Preview of E melodic minor

The E melodic minor scale in one octave

Notated below is a one octave scale of the key of E *melodic minor*. See the preceeding section on the structure of scales for a review of how the melodic minor scale is constructed.

E = tonic*   B = dominant**

(**Tonic* is the term for the <u>first</u> and main note and chord of a key.)
(** *Dominant* is the term for the <u>fifth</u> note and chord of a key.)

The E melodic minor scale in the 1st position

The notes C and D are "sharped" in the ascending, and lowered, using naturals, in the descending scale motion.

Tonic and dominant chords of the key of E minor

The E minor chord (notes = E, G, B) is the *tonic* chord built on the first tone of the E minor scale.

The B major chord (notes = B, D#, F#) is the *dominant* chord built on the fifth tone of the E minor scale.

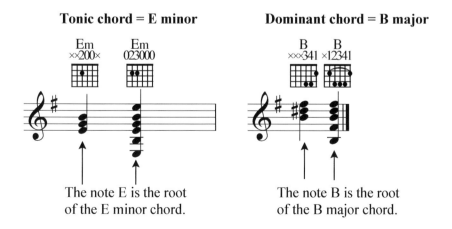

Tonic chord = E minor

The note E is the root of the E minor chord.

Dominant chord = B major

The note B is the root of the B major chord.

Key of E minor
8 short exercises

Scale

Melodic Thirds

Chords

Arpeggios

Thirds

Sixths

Octaves

Tenths

Bourrée
from Lute Suite # 1 BWV 996

This is a duet arrangement of Bach's famous Bourrée in E minor from the 1st lute suite.
After learning the melody of the first part, listen to how the bass melody of the 2nd part
is not only a great tune by itself, but also perfectly accompanies the main melody above.

JOHANN SEBASTIAN BACH

(1685-1750)

As you learn both parts, over time, while playing one part, seek to imagine the sound
of the part you are <u>not</u> playing: it is a matter of training the inner ear, and once you
can truly hear two musical lines with equal clarity, you will find that your technical
skill of playing the guitar naturally grows alongside the development of your inner hearing.

The Three Ravens

Ravenscroft was a composer of psalm-tunes and other church music
and also the author of a musical treatise.

THOMAS RAVENSCROFT
(1593-1635)

Minuet

Robert de Visée, in his <u>Livre de pièces pour la Guittare</u> (1686), writes of his desire to
*"conform to the taste of skillful people, in giving my pieces, as far as my weak
talents permit, the flavour of those of the inimitable monsieur de Lully."*

ROBERT DE VISÉE
(c. 1660-1724)

Prelude

from Method for the Guitar, Opus 59

Allegro

MATTEO CARCASSI
(1792-1853)

Etude

Op. 60 # XIV

FERNANDO SOR
(1778-1839)

Andante

Romance

I wrote this piece many years ago for beginners in the very first stages of their
guitar skills. It is of course related to the famous *Romance D'amour*.

This is offered as a kind of introductory etude. It uses the same key and arpeggio pattern as the
Romance D'amour, but lacks any difficult bar techniques.

JEFFREY GOODMAN

Leymön Tendrel

I have only heard this exquisite Tibetan Buddhist melody sung acapella. It is by
Rigdzin Jigme Lingpa (1730-1798) and is deeply devotional in intent. The melody
itself is to be played very freely and without strong accent. The harmonizations
lightly accentuate the melodic design.

ANCIENT TIBETAN MELODY

Chapter 23

Key of D major

This chapter introduces the key of D major. D major is a key rich in great repertoire, not only within the classical genre, but throughout popular music as well. Vivaldi's Concerto in D for guitar and strings, Rodrigo's Concierto de Aranjuez, and music by Bach, Albeniz, Sor, and Villa Lobos are representative of the music guitarists play in the key of D major.

This chapter contains:

Preview of D major

Eight short exercises

A duet by Henry Purcell

Solo repertoire by Sanz, De Visée, Dowland, and Fuhrmann

Preview of D major

The D major scale in one octave

Notated below is a one octave scale of the key of D *major*.

tonic*   dominant**

(*Tonic* is the term for the <u>first</u> and main note and chord of a key.)
(** *Dominant* is the term for the <u>fifth</u> note and chord of a key.)

Notes of the D major scale in the 1st position

Tonic and dominant chords of the key of D major

The D major chord (notes = D, F#, A) is the *tonic* chord built on the 1st tone of the D major scale.
The A major chord (notes = A, C#, E) is the *dominant* chord built on the 5th tone of the D major scale.

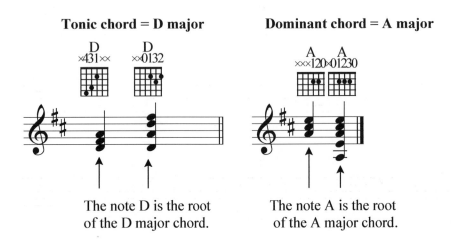

Tonic chord = D major   Dominant chord = A major

The note D is the root   The note A is the root
of the D major chord.   of the A major chord.

Key of D major
8 short exercises

Scale

Melodic Thirds

Chords

Arpeggios

Thirds

Sixths

Octaves

Tenths

Rigaudon

Purcell was an English composer and organist of Westminster Abbey.
He is said to have died as a result of a cold he caught after being
locked out of his own home on a stormy winter night.

HENRY PURCELL
(1658-1695)

Stately

Guitar I plays in 2nd position for the rest of the piece:

Torneo

GASPAR SANZ
(1640-1710)

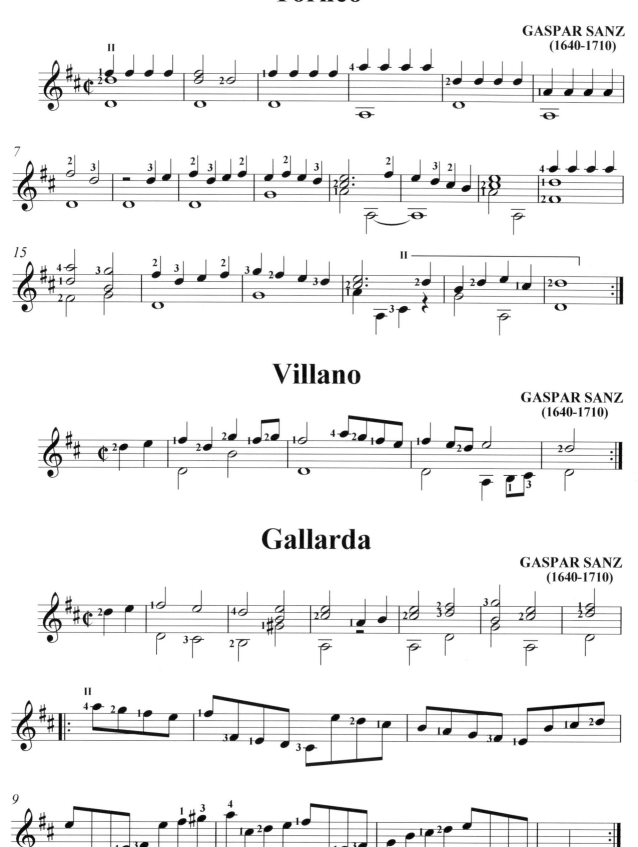

Villano

GASPAR SANZ
(1640-1710)

Gallarda

GASPAR SANZ
(1640-1710)

Rujero

Sanz was born at Calanda, Aragon, Spain. He later studied guitar in Rome
and became teacher to Don Juan of Austria. All pieces of Sanz included
in our book are from his <u>Instrucción de música sobre la Guitarra Española</u> (1697).
The Spanish composer Joaquin Rodrigo used Sanz' music as inspiration
for his *Fantasia Para un Gentilhombre* composed for Andrés Segovia.

GASPAR SANZ
(1640-1710)

Paradetas

GASPAR SANZ
(1640-1710)

Soldier's Joy

TRADITIONAL
(fiddle tune)

Allegro

The left hand plays in 2nd position throughout this piece.

The Parlement
originally for lute

(The notation: **6=D** means to tune
the 6th string down to the note D.)

ANONYMOUS
(16th Century)

6=D

Minuet
from the Suite in D minor

De Visée composed this for the 5-course baroque guitar.

ROBERT DE VISÉE
(c. 1660-1724)

Orlando Sleepeth

Dowland, English lutenist and composer, served the King of Denmark and
other royal patrons, but never was appointed to the court of Queen Elizabeth.

JOHN DOWLAND
(1563-1626)

Tanz

Fuhrmann was a German Lutenist and composer who lived in Nürnberg during the 1600's.
His works can be found in the *Testudo Gallico-Germanico*.

This lively dance, transcribed from the lute, is played in the 2nd position throughout.
The right hand thumb plays all the bass notes.

GEORG FUHRMANN
(17th Century)

Chapter 24

Key of A major

This chapter introduces the key of A major. A major is one of the most popular keys among composers and guitarists. One reason for this is that the three open bass strings are tuned to the tonic (A), subdominant* (D), and dominant (E) pitches of the scale. This gives composers great latitude in creating music that is idiomatic for the guitar.

This chapter contains:

Preview of A major

Eight short exercises

A duet by Jean-Baptiste Besarde

Solo repertoire by De Visée, Mozart, anonymous 19th century Hungarian dances, and a 16th century Elizabethan lute piece

*The music theory term "subdominant" refers to the fourth note of the scale and the chord built with that note as the root.

Preview of A major

The A major scale in one octave

Notated below is a one octave scale of the key of A *major*.

tonic*   dominant**

(*_Tonic_ is the term for the <u>first</u> and main note and chord of a key.)
(** _Dominant_ is the term for the <u>fifth</u> note and chord of a key.)

Notes of the A major scale in the 1st and 2nd positions

Tonic and dominant chords of the key of A major

The A major chord (notes = A, C#, E) is the *tonic* chord built on the 1st tone of the A major scale.
The E major chord (notes = E, G#, B) is the *dominant* chord built on the 5th tone of the A major scale.

Tonic chord = A minor   Dominant chord = E major

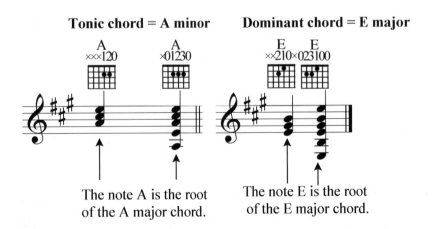

The note A is the root   The note E is the root
of the A major chord.   of the E major chord.

Key of A major
8 short exercises

Scale

Melodic Thirds

Chords

A   F#m   D   Bm   E   A

Arpeggios

Thirds

Sixths

Octaves

Tenths

Branle de Village

Besarde was a Burgundian lutenist and composer.
In addition to music he studied law and medicine.
His Thesaurus harmonicus and Novus partus
are sources of not only his music but also many
other composers of his time.

JEAN-BAPTISTE BESARDE
(1567-1625)

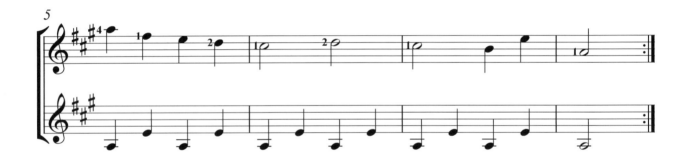

Two Hungarian Folk Songs

I

II

Minuet
"Livre de Pièces pour la Guittarre" (1686)

The 17th century guitarist and lutenist Robert de Visée served as chamber musician to Louis XIV. Accounts of his life record that he often played guitar for the Dauphin, and in the evenings would at times play for the king at his bedside.

Among his most famous collections is his <u>Livre de Pièces pour la Guittarre</u> originally published in 1686.

This short Minuet in A major is one of the most beautiful in the collection.
Its simplicity and elegance beckon the guitarist to play with clarity
and lightness of touch in order to reflect the refinement of the music.

ROBERT DE VISÉE
(c. 1660-1724)

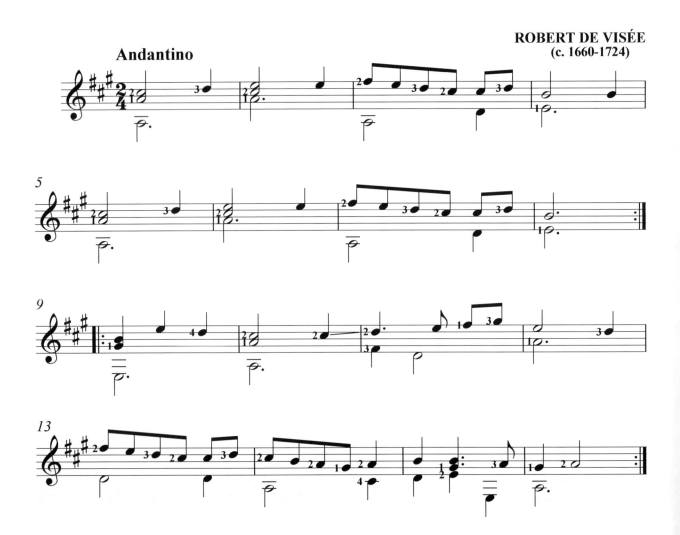

Wilson's Wilde

Elizabethan lute piece

ANONYMOUS
(16th century)

Allegretto

Theme
from the Piano Sonata in A Major, K. 331

This is an arrangement for guitar of the
famous theme of Mozart's Piano Sonata in A major.

WOLFGANG AMADEUS MOZART
(1756-1791)

Chapter 25

Key of E major

This chapter introduces the key of E major. E major is in some ways the most popular key to compose in for the guitar. Among the reasons for this is the tuning of the first and sixth strings to the note E. Whether you are playing a Bach lute suite, a Dowland fantasie, a Beatles tune or a Rolling Stones rock classic, the key of E major offers virtually unlimited choices for the guitarist to explore.

This chapter contains:

        Preview of E major

        Eight short exercises

        A duet by J. S. Bach from the 6th Cello suite

        Solo repertoire by Sor, Carcassi, Aguado, and a 17th century lute piece

Preview of E major

The E major scale in one octave

Notated below is a one octave scale of the key of E *major*.

E = tonic* B = dominant**

(*Tonic* is the term for the <u>first</u> and main note and chord of a key.)
(** *Dominant* is the term for the <u>fifth</u> note and chord of a key.)

E major scale in the first position

Tonic and dominant chords of the key of E major

The E major chord (notes = E, G#, B) is the *tonic* chord built on the 1st tone of the E major scale.

The B major chord (notes = B, D#, F#) is the *dominant* chord built on the 5th tone of the E major scale.

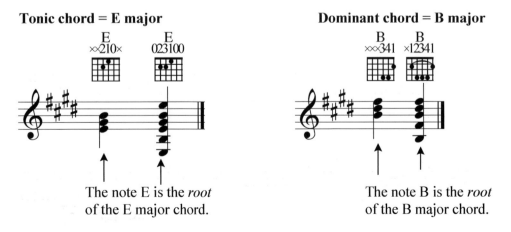

Tonic chord = E major

The note E is the *root* of the E major chord.

Dominant chord = B major

The note B is the *root* of the B major chord.

Key of E major

8 short exercises

Scale

Melodic Thirds

Chords

Arpeggios

Thirds

Sixths

Octaves

Tenths

Gavotte II
from Cello Suite # 6 BWV 1012

The 6th Cello Suite of Bach, originally in the key of D major, contains many movements that transcribe idiomatically to the guitar. Andrés Segovia made this gavotte a frequent encore piece for his recitals.

JOHANN SEBASTIAN BACH
(1685-1750)

Etude in E major

Opus 60 # XV

Follow the right hand fingering suggestions carefully. Also explore
your own ideas and experiment until you find solutions that enhance
the musical intent of each phrase.

FERNANDO SOR
(1778-1839)

Englesa
from the original for lute

Notice how the meter changes from 4/4 time to 3/4 time after the second
repeated section. This was a common variation technique during the renaissance.

ANONYMOUS
(17th century)

D.C al Fine

Prelude in E major

from <u>Method for the Guitar</u>, Opus 59

MATTEO CARCASSI
(1791-1853)

Etude in E major
lesson #38 from *New Guitar Method*

Dionisio Aguado, along with his friend Fernando Sor, were the 19th centuries'
two finest composers for the guitar. Both wrote and published guitar method books
that have much to offer even today, more than 150 years after their initial publication.

The etude offered here is from Aguado's *New Guitar Method*, initially printed
in Spain in 1843. Andrés Segovia recorded this etude along with seven others from
Aguado's method. This etude, for all its apparent simplicity, is melodically subtle
and in order to have it sound at its best, should be played with a light touch and
careful sustaining of all the quarter notes.

Aguado wrote of musical expression, *"The sublime aspect of the art, as far as the musician is
concerned, lies in giving true feeling to musical compositions, expressing in the
instrument the ideas of the composer in such a way that the sounds transcend the mere
ear and move the heart of the listeners."*

DIONISIO AGUADO
(1784-1849)

Chapter 26

Key of F major

This chapter introduces the key of F major. In contrast ot the keys of A, D and E major, the key of F is difficult to compose for and awkward to play in. Even so, the harmonic domain of F frequently occurs as a region within pieces in other keys. For example, the Cappricio Arabe by Tarrega has a section written in the key area of F major, even though the piece is primarily in the key of D minor.

This chapter contains:

Preview of F major

Eight short exercises

A duet by Handel

Solo repertoire by Handel, Campian, Mozart, Diabelli, Mertz and Sor

Preview of F major

The F major scale in one octave

Notated below is a one octave scale of the key of F major.

F = tonic*   C = dominant**

(*Tonic* is the term for the <u>first</u> and main note and chord of a key.)
(** *Dominant* is the term for the <u>fifth</u> note and chord of a key.)

Notes of the F major scale in the first position

Tonic and dominant chords of the key of F major

The F major chord (notes = F, A, C) is the *tonic* chord built on the 1st tone of the F major scale.

The C major chord (notes = C, E, G) is the *dominant* chord built on the 5th tone of the F major scale.

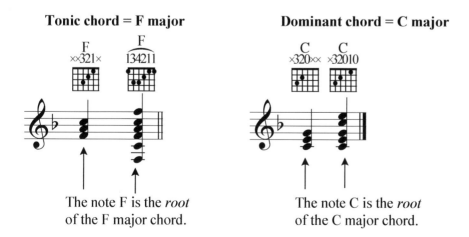

Tonic chord = F major   **Dominant chord = C major**

The note F is the *root*   The note C is the *root*
of the F major chord.   of the C major chord.

Key of F major
8 short exercises

Gavotte

"Handel, to him I bow the knee."
Ludwig van Beethoven

GEORG FRIEDRICH HANDEL
(1685-1759)

Moderato

Gavotte

Here is a solo guitar transcription of the duet on the previous page.
Although not written orignially for lute or guitar, this tuneful gavotte by Handel
works well for solo guitar.

GEORG FRIEDRICH HANDEL
(1685-1759)

The Peaceful Western Wind
Elizabethan Song

Campian composed over 100 songs for voice and lute
and was also a lawyer and physician.

THOMAS CAMPIAN
(1562-1620)

Minuet

*"I pay no attention whatever to anyone's praise or blame....
I simply follow my own feelings."* W. A. Mozart

WOLFGANG AMADEUS MOZART
(1756-1791)

Menuett

Anton Diabelli was a pianist, guitarist
and composer who was a student of Haydn.

ANTON DIABELLI
(1781-1858)

Maestoso

Mertz was a Hungarian guitarist and
composer who eventually setteled in Vienna
and became guitarist of the Empress.

JOHANN KASPAR MERTZ
(1806-1856)

Etude in F Major

Opus 31 # XI

Sor's Maxim #2 *"To require more
from skill than from strength."*

FERNANDO SOR
(1778-1839)

Chapter 27

Key of D minor

This chapter introduces the key of D minor. D minor is an especially expressive key on the guitar. Spanning the Renaissance, Baroque, Classical and Romantic periods, music in D minor gives guitarists a lifetime of potentials of musical exploration. Among the works vital to the guitar repertoire are lute pieces of Dowland and Weiss, Bach's Chaconne, and guitar works of Sor, Tarrega, Castelnuovo Tedesco and Brouwer.

This chapter contains:

Preview of D minor

Eight short exercises

Duets by Corelli and Bach

Solo repertoire by Carcassi, Purcell, Corelli, and Sanz

Preview D melodic minor

The D melodic minor scale in one octave

Notated below is a one octave scale of the key of D *melodic minor*.

tonic*   dominant**

(*Tonic is the term for the <u>first</u> and main note and chord of a key.)
(** Dominant is the term for the <u>fifth</u> note and chord of a key.)

Notes of the D melodic minor scale in the 1st position

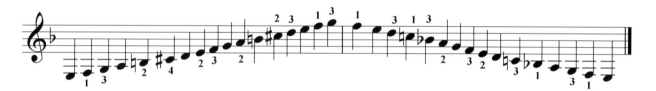

Tonic and dominant chords of the key of D melodic minor

The D minor chord (notes = D, F, A) is the *tonic* chord built on the 1st tone of the D minor scale.
The A major chord (notes = A, C#, E) is the *dominant* chord built on the 5th tone of the D minor scale.

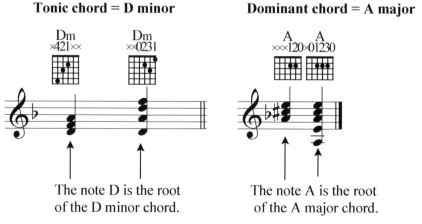

Tonic chord = D minor

The note D is the root
of the D minor chord.

Dominant chord = A major

The note A is the root
of the A major chord.

Key of D minor
8 Short exercises

Scale

Melodic Thirds

Chords

Arpeggios

Thirds

Sixths

Octaves

Tenths

Gavotte

Arcangelo Corelli, Italian violinist, was one of the great composers of the Baroque period.
When playing this simple gavotte, focus on making the quarter note motion in
both parts synchronize precisely. Also, by carefully observing the rests at the
end of each phrase unit, it will help to create a stately and elegant effect of the dance.

ARCANGELO CORELLI
(1653-1717)

Prelude in D Minor
from *Complete Method for Guitar, Opus 59*

*"Arpeggios as used on the guitar produce an agreeable effect, and, as studies,
give strength and agility to the fingers of the right hand."* Matteo Carcassi

Andantino

MATTEO CARCASSI
(1792-1853)

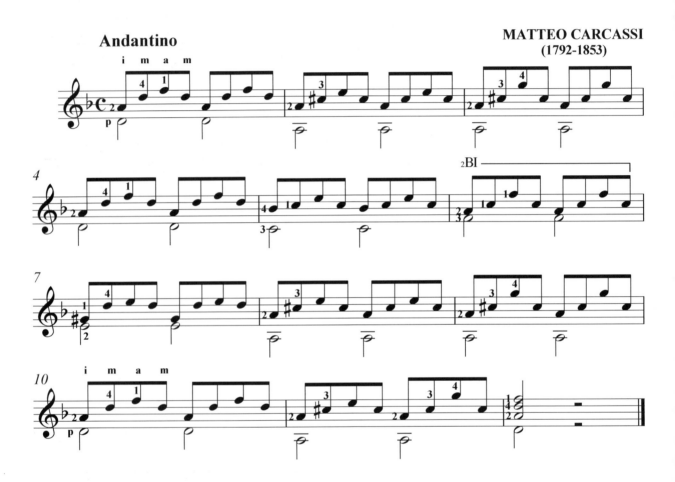

Hungarian Dance

Allegretto

ANONYMOUS
(19th Century)

Renaissance Dance
from original for lute

ANONYMOUS
(late 1600's)

Maestoso

Minuet

*"The Author has no more to add, but his hearty wishes, that
his Book may fall into no other hands but theirs who carry Musical Souls
about them..."* Henry Purcell, from Preface to Sonatas in III Parts.

HENRY PURCELL
(1658-1695)

Andantino

Fine

D.C. al Fine

La Folia

Corelli's "La Folia" became a popular theme for composers to write their own variations on.

ARCANGELO CORELLI
(1653-1713)

Folías

Gaspar Sanz adapted Corelli's theme to produce his own setting for guitar.
In Sanz' original this theme is followed by a set of variations.

GASPAR SANZ
(1640-1710)

Crab Canon
from the Musical Offering, BWV 1079

Bach wrote this piece in 1749 after his famous visit to Frederick the Great of Prussia. Frederick is said to have written the theme that begins in Guitar I. After a long and difficult journey to the court Frederick gave Bach this theme and asked Bach to improvise upon it. Bach improvised with consumate mastery and great acclaim, and, after returning home, he composed the Musical Offering, which, of course, was dedicated to Frederick. This canon is called a "crab canon" because the 2nd part is the same as the 1st part, but written backwards.

JOHANN SEBASTIAN BACH
(1685-1750)

The double line marks where the canon plays backwards. It makes a perfect musical "mirror".

Chapter 28

Flamenco

In this chapter you will be introduced to a few of the basic concepts and notations for flamenco guitar music. Keep in mind that flamenco guitar is a whole world unto itself, and should you be inclined, today there are extensive resources for your exploration of flamenco style. There are many excellent instruction books that are devoted to all aspects of playing flamenco. Also there are superb collections of solo flamenco pieces by such masters as Sabicas, Juan Serrano, and Paco de Lucia.

This chapter contains:

An introductory guide to basic flamenco strums and notation

Three solo flamenco pieces - Malaguena, Tientos and Soleares

Flamenco notation and strumming

The historical origins of flamenco music are obscure. But the music itself is one of the most beguiling and exciting styles ever created for guitar. What I offer here are a few of the flamenco pieces that my students have found inspiring and accessible. My own teacher Theodore Norman collected flamenco music in Spain in the 1950's by asking gypsies playing in local cafés if he could write down their improvisations. Malagueña, Tientos and Soleares are traditional arrangements drawn from the many sources I have encountered over the years.

Flamenco Notation

In flamenco the notation of pitch and rhythm is the same as classical music.

Flamenco has a variety of special strumming techniques that require special notation. All of the other notation for left and right hands are the same as for classical. For the Right Hand we sometimes use the small or "pinky" finger in strumming. The symbol for the small finger is the letter "s".

Basic rule # 1: For simple down and up strumming always use the index (i) finger *unless* there is a notation for another finger to be used.

Basic rule #2: Most often strums on downbeats (eg: on 1 2 3 & 4) are played "down" from bass to treble, and strums on upbeats (eg: the **&** of 1 **&** 2 **&** 3 **&**) are played "up" from treble to bass notes.

Flamenco Strumming

Simple strums: 1. The letter "*i*" means to use the index finger (*i*) to strum across the chord notes.
2. The letter "*p*" means to use the thumb (*p*) to strum across the chord notes.

Direction of strum: The arrowhead symbol (see below) indicates the musical direction of the strum: that is either:

   1. from the bass note up to the highest sounding pitch,
or 2. from the highest note down to the bass:

Strum from bass to treble.   Strum from treble to bass .   Strum towards the floor   Strum towards the ceiling

Compare the music notated to the right of these measures: both passages are identical, with the arrows substituting for the chords written above.

When the chord notes remain the same, the "arrows" mean to play the same notes as the initial chord. At the beginning of any new bar the chord notes are always written out.

Rasgueado is the characteristic strumming that gives flamenco its identity. There are many variants of this strum, and every gypsy plays even the "same" strum with his own individual flair.

When you see this notation: ^{sami} it means to strum the strings beginning with the R.H. small finger (s), followed by the ring finger (a), then the middle finger (m), and then the index finger (i).

Over time this will become a smooth motion of all the fingers moving together, kind of like dominos when they are stacked and then fall. It helps if you play with a light touch, just skimming the back of the fingernails across the strings. Keep the hand perpendicular to the strings so the fingers do not get "caught up" on the strings as they pass over the chord notes:

Malagueña

Tientos

Soleares

4497807

Made in the USA
Charleston, SC
31 January 2010